To Karin
Blessings

Less Than An Eagle, More Than A Duck & Other Stuff

Open the gift of each new day with joyous expectation. Who knows, you just might fly with eagles.

Mildred Dennis

Mildred Dennis

authorHOUSE®

AuthorHouse™
1663 Liberty Drive
Bloomington, IN 47403
www.authorhouse.com
Phone: 1-800-839-8640

Published by AuthorHouse 5/10/2013

ISBN: 978-1-4817-4812-4 (sc)
ISBN: 978-1-4817-4813-1 (hc)
ISBN: 978-1-4817-4811-7 (e)

Library of Congress Control Number: 2013907754

Interior photos: Pages 57, 58 Rick Dennis; 85 Caton's Grove Church; 105, 110, 113
Author; 118 Donna Skufca and Author; 119 Mama; 125 Author and Daddy; 127
Sister June (Keene) and Author, 141 Author and husband James. All Family Photos

Bible References, Good News Bible, American Bible Society, 1976

This book is printed on acid-free paper.

Dedication

With grateful thanks to
Pastor Bill Grant
Who has encouraged me to fly with eagles
While trusting in the sure love of God

PART ONE

—

God's Natural World

Winter's Crystal Moments

Living along the shores of Lake Erie in Northeast Ohio has pluses and minuses in the winter season. An Alberta Clipper can pile snow on your doorstep, while one of those storms sweeping up from the Oklahoma/Texas panhandle can leave drifts waist deep--too deep, too cold!

Time was when I would mush out with the dogs, but no more. Now I rarely venture far from the comfort of a crackling fire. With slipping and sliding, shoveling and shivering, winter now seems to hold few delights. Yet I recently discovered the season can offer a few crystal moments to be treasured.

One afternoon I found myself trudging across a snow-covered meadow at the bottom of a hill. (Don't ask me why.) One other set of tracks almost obscured by the most recent flakes traced along in front of me. I stopped, alone, and as I looked around, it was as if I surely had stumbled across God's storehouse of snows.

The silence was only an illusion. As I listened closely, the creek trickled between frozen edges as it hurried to a rendezvous with greater waters. A branch snapped beneath the weight of some venturesome winter critter. The snow birds began a melody—a call here, an answer there—and it seemed the trees were filled with their singing.

Cued by the overture, a fantasy snow ballet began. Great soft flakes appeared, dipping and swirling, kissing my upturned cheeks; then waltzing to the earth. It was a special time lifted from an ordinary day, as all nature celebrated a late afternoon's moment in the meadow. I hugged myself as a feeling of warmth touched my soul.

I remembered another night, with snow drifting waist high around the house. My white sled dogs were almost lost as they leaped from drift to drift surely answering a call from their northern ancestors. Then they would stand quite still, tracing the path of each falling flake, before racing away again. The thrill of their happiness stirred my memory chimes again and a little boy came running.

It was a spring season and he came pushing against a strong March wind—windmill arms turning, sturdy legs pumping—shouting, "Good news! Good news! Mama, come and see."

I followed him to a flower bed tangled with last year's growth. He got down on his grubby knees and in his little hands gently cradled the first daffodil of the season. "See, Mama, good news."

As I pulled away from the spring memory, I began pushing the snow ahead of me with my boots, making my way back home. As a pursuer of summer days I thought, "How often we seek what we can't possibly have at the moment and miss so many gifts that God wishes for us."

Home was in sight but not quite there, before another memory tugged. Christmas had just passed. Wasn't it in another field where the angels announced to the shepherds, "Behold I bring you *good news* of a Savior born in Bethlehem, who shall be called Jesus. He is Christ the Lord,"--a priceless gift for the ages.

How much more could be our joy of living, if we would just open up and flow with the seasons like the "beasts and the children."

The gift of Good News is yours waiting to be discovered.

Only God Can Give A Sunrise

Sometimes I think if I were asked to choose only one gift from God's nature chest to fill the yearning in my soul, it would be the *rising* sun. Each dawn speaks to the hope of the new-born day in tones shaded by the seasons.

The **Winter** sunrise edges across a frozen harlequin landscape--black branches etched against white snow. The purple shadows of night slowly retreat, leaving pink trail markers across the fields of diamonds. The midnight storm has moved on, and as the sun brands its circle into the blue of day, its warmth belies the surrounding chill.

Breathless anticipation is the theme of the birds' overture to the **Spring** sunrise. Lazy sky riders trade their gray mantles for soft peach and lemon yellow ponchos. The ever-brightening scene reveals an expectant earth reborn--tiny green leaves uncurling, flower-petal faces stretching to the east--awaiting the life-giving touch of the rays. My face, too, is drawn upward to the warmth.

Surely the **Summer** sunrises to be savored are endless--those from my patio, on the beach, or near a mountain top--but I believe my personal favorite can be found while sitting, pole in hand, at the edge of a fishing pond.

First, the predawn silence surrounds the scene and quiets the soul. Then, as the wind rises, the steel-grey calm of the pond begins to ripple into glittering silver. The cattle begin to stir as suddenly the sunrise artist splashes the canvas with color--changing, slipping, sliding blues, purples, oranges, mauves, yellows. Savor the scene quickly, for all too soon the colors become a fire ball surrounded by endless blue. Another blazing day on the prairie has begun.

Sunrises in **Autumn** come in brilliant scenes, but few could rival the panorama that unrolled on my way to school a few years ago. There is a high point on Route 44 South where the tip of the rising sun tops a growth of trees. What has been an illusion of darkness becomes an expanse of golden nuggets dancing across velvet russets and reds. Truly a vision to be remembered as I caught my breath, then drove on.

Just another sunrise singing a psalm to the glory of the Creator who gives, not only the sunrises, but all the gifts of nature. He asks only that, as the caretakers. we treasure them all for the priceless gifts they are.

Chasing Fireflies

A very special memory of Oklahoma spring evenings is going out to the lake with Daddy. He would plug his way around the edge of the lake with all the other 'after work' fishermen, to lure the bass coming out for an evening snack.

I played with the other kids on the beach. No matter what games we came up with, every evening ended the same way. As soon as the sun dropped into the western end of the lake, the gathering darkness flashed with hundreds of lightenin' bugs in staccato flight.

We had our mayonnaise jars with holes already punched in the lids. The race was on. Who could catch enough flashing lights to fill their jar first? (Nobody ever 'filled' their jar.)

After the heat of the sun, the cool wind felt good as we flung ourselves into the acres of glowing green-gold lanterns. As the darkness spread from the woods to the beach, the risks grew.

Brambles snatched at bare skin, fallen branches flew up and barked the shins and sometimes the lake moved right into a pathway. All of these happenings could put the precious glowing jar in jeopardy.

As the bass went back to their hidden hollows, the fishermen drifted to the beach fire to have a cup of coffee and exchange brags about the "granddaddy of them all" yet to be caught; or how he'd been hooked but just slipped off.

We kids stayed just outside the circle of the fire, with the jars lined up in a row. I still remember their beauty--glowing, fascinating, but how deceiving they were. I always felt cheated as I opened the lid to let the fireflies free. They gave no warmth against the night chill, no light for my path. Still, the next time Daddy went to plug for the bass, I went along to chase lightenin' bugs with the other kids.

Life has many firefly experiences. Sometimes I chase them. Yet, when I catch them to put in my jar, I still feel disappointment for the warmth and light is only a promise--unfulfilled.

Everyday Rainbows

One Spring evening, Donna came rushing into the house shouting, "Come and look! Come quick! There's a double rainbow in the sky!"

Sure enough. There in the eastern sky was not one, but two complete rainbows, and they were spanning all the way horizon to horizon. That's something to get the attention. One seldom sees a double rainbow; and even one usually fades before reaching the ground. Not so this time. The colors of each bow seemed to glow from the rays of the western sun.

Donna rushed around looking for the camera, but by the time she found it, the rainbows were almost gone. Rainbows come and rainbows go, leaving only a memory of their beauty.

The story of the great rainbow is well-known but most people seem to focus more on Noah and the great FLOOD. They remember Noah building an ark to prepare for the rain, even though he didn't know much about an ark and had never seen 'rain'. Then the animals started coming two by two and Noah's family enters the picture, and we start to wonder how all this is going to work. But they all got in the ark and **didn't it rain!**

My favorite part of the story is what came afterward. The rain stopped, and there was **the** rainbow. (Another wonder Noah had yet to see.) The bow was set, a covenant was made, and God said, "I do set my bow in the cloud, and the earth will never be destroyed by water again."

Each time I see these lovely colors, I think of a different promise. They all hold a meaning for me in my relationship with God.

I start on the earth side and work upward--*indigo* and *violet*. I put these two colors together because for me they are the royal colors, the colors of the King. Timothy says, "He's the King eternal. The King of Kings. The Lord of Lords."

I know that if my life is to be filled with the greatest possible meaning, then it must be lived with this King at the heart of all my actions. No matter how busy or how calm, I continually find myself saying, "Hey, Lord, Where do we go from here?"

Of course, you know, I haven't always followed this plan. The King was with me, but at different times (especially in the early years), I nodded to him only casually. I could do most things by myself, so I thought. I didn't consciously keep him out; I just didn't invite him in.

Gradually, I realized an emptiness was invading the 'fullness' of my living. One day, the answer came. God's gift for the world was meant for me, too. All the parts of my life took on new meaning as the 'reality' of Christ became a 'reality' for me. He is the King. He does know the way and He can get us through if we're not too stubborn or too proud to go along with Him. So we have indigo and violet for a Royal Partner that's yearns to travel with us.

The next color is *blue*, the color of the boundless sky. For me, it's the color of God's boundless love. I don't know that I can think of anything about love that hasn't been written or said.

I think maybe John said it best when he urged us, "Dear friends, let us love one another, for love comes from God."

There are so many facets of love. That between a husband and wife, a parent and child, friend and friend, neighbor and neighbor and then it starts getting a little tricky. It's even possible to feel love for a stranger. But the greatest of loves is the one between the Lord and His creation. Paul reminds us that, "Nothing can separate us from God's love." If you just believe this, anything is possible.

The next color is *green*. Since moving to Northeast Ohio, I've come to cherish green. The beauty of the trees in spring is a green unequaled and with their rebirth, I have continual hope. Sometimes it may grow a little faint, but as Peter said, "God gave us new life by raising Jesus Christ from the dead. This fills us with living hope."

When we get hit with a barb of despair, we can lie there and moan.

But does that mean we have to lie there forever? No! Get up! Get back on the road and do it with hope.

Now let's look at *yellow*. There's only one possible choice, we must think of the sun. And I can't think of the sun without thinking of joy. It's the color of action. Again, our friend Peter said, "Rejoice with joy unspeakable and full of glory." What a glorious thought--joy unspeakable.

Honestly, I'm not sure I've ever been so full of joy that I couldn't speak. But then, hardly anything keeps me from speaking.

The gospels are filled with words of joy and I've always found it hard to understand why so many people equate living a Christian life with living a life of gloom. Maybe it's something handed down from our forefathers. I don't know.

But I challenge you. Put a little joy in your life because you know what, just knowing the Lord is a joyful thing.

What about the next color, *orange*? I see the fire of faith as kindled by the Holy Spirit. At one time, I had some problems with this Holy Spirit and how it fit into the scheme of things. As time has passed, I can now begin to see the purpose of the Holy Spirit in God's plan for my life.

Certainly those who were present when the Holy Spirit came with 'tongues of fire' had a reason to be excited about their faith. We should be so excited!

Paul says, "To have a faith is to be sure of things we hope for, to be certain of things we cannot see." To be sure! To be certain!

Isn't that what we need for day-to-day living? It's right there in front of us if we take off the blinders. The truth is, sureness really can be ours. I've seen it. Sometimes, I've known it. Why don't you warm yourself at this fire? The orange of faith is a vital color of the rainbow for all.

The last color, found on the heaven side of the bow--*red*. The most obvious choice to represent red is His blood. I see the precious savior's blood which bought our salvation and set us free. It may be difficult for us to understand about blood sacrifices, but it was the custom of the time.

Jesus went to the cross because it was God's will; a way of providing eternal salvation for His children. We SERVE a living God. Sometimes, the problem seems to be that we want to be served--not serve.

Lord, help us to remember that the rainbow ends with red; red for his for his precious blood.

Yes, the rainbow is now complete. We have a King who gives us love, filled with hope, so that we can serve in joy and faith, that promises us salvation. But we also have a King who leaves the choice to us. Do we want to choose this promise?

A rainbow doesn't happen every day. There are two necessary items. One is the rain and the other is the sun. If it were left to me, the sun would shine every day. But God knows we need the rain for all living things to grow. Sometimes there's storms along the way, but it's the sun shining through the rain that forms the bow.

As every child knows, there's one more part of a rainbow and that's the legendary pot of gold at the end. My rainbow has no pot of gold. It has something finer than gold. For at my rainbow's end there is the joy of living for today and life eternal for tomorrow

God said, "I set my bow in the sky as a promise." God's promises are true yesterday, today, and tomorrow. Why not choose to be a part of the rainbow promise?

Only A Rabbit

I'm still giving thought as to exactly how that rabbit came to live at our house. I surely don't remember saying "Yes," to the question of his coming. Actually, I don't even remember his coming. Donna sort of slipped him in on my blind side, and there he was.

There was nothing spectacular about him except to Donna. His color was sort of a mingling of brown and grey and soft beige fur, which suggested a number of ancestors.

Lots of names were tossed around and I seem to remember Tumbleweeds as the final choice, but I never heard that name used and Bunne was the name he "answered" to. (I think Donna thought the 'e' rather than a 'y' gave a touch of elegance to a rather ordinary rabbit.)

Each of us took note of him once in awhile. We laughed at the funny way he wiggled his nose, ate the bits of clover in the grass, or stretched up tall to reach an offered carrot. Occasionally, I would even reach out and marvel at the softness of his fur.

But, no question, he was Donna's. She built the pen, she bought the food and fed him faithfully twice a day, she sheltered him against the winter snow, she talked to him, played with him and maybe most important of all, she loved him.

Then one morning, she found him so still and so cold, and she cried. Some might say, "But it was only a rabbit. What's the big deal?"

It's a hard thing to say goodbye to a friend, and for Donna, Bunne had been a good friend. The tears seemed to help wash away a little of the hurt.

It seems to me that to love always opens the heart to many emotions--

one of these is sure to be deep sadness. But not to love. . . not to love could only be to live in a void of darkness.

Even though it means she is sure to stumble at times against the rocks of hurt, I'm so grateful that Donna chooses to walk the way of love.

PART TWO

—

Faith — A Daily Walk

The Butterfly Girl

From the window I watched the little girl rolling around in the grass; such joy came bubbling out of her laughter. Ok, I wonder what has her attention now? Then I saw it,--the great Monarch butterfly flitting along the top of the hedge. Seeing what fun she was having, I turned back to my chores.

It wasn't long till I heard her cries, "Mama, come out here! Quick, come now!"

I hurried out the door and there she sat with tears trailing down her dusty face. She sobbed, "He's all broke, Mama, he's all broke." Donna opened her tiny fist. There lay the butterfly with the beautiful wings crushed into pieces.

"I just wanted to keep him. You gotta' fix him Mama, fix him."

I held her close and wiped her tears, but how do you explain this to a three-year-old? Mamas can't fix a broken butterfly, it's just not possible.

Later that day while I doing some ironing (a great time for creative thinking), I thought about the broken butterfly--how like the fragile ways of love--touch it lightly, treat it gently and it is ever present. Clutch it tightly and it will be crushed into pieces and sift away through empty fingers.

It was many years later that suddenly the butterfly girl popped into my mind again, and I thought, "Hm, I think there's another way to look at this broken butterfly.

"All broke!" I think surely most of us have something in our life that is *all broke*. Sometimes no matter how hard we try, we tend to think that like the butterfly, there's no way to mend the brokenness, so we just hold it tight in our fist--and crush it more.

This isn't a unique reaction; we find many of the faithful throughout the Bible who held on tight to 'broken wings.'

Take Sarah. After she and Abraham were married, she was desperate to give him a son. She tried a lot of things but time went on and no baby came. She clutched her dream in her hand, till one day an angel came to her and said, "Sarah, don't be afraid. You will have a son very soon."

Sarah laughed right in the angel's face 'cause she was now 90 years old. She thought, "Surely you must be out of your mind." Still, she dared to open her hand and God touched her dream. With the birth of Isaac, Sarah became the mother of the nation Israel.

Let's take a look at Gideon, hiding in the wine press as he threshes the wheat. He is hiding because the Midianites have taken over the country and, as happened so often in the old Testament days, Israel was a defeated nation. Surely Gideon must have clung to a dream of doing *something* for his people; but when the angel of the Lord appeared in that winepress and called out, "Gideon! The Lord has called you to save Israel." you think maybe Gideon was startled? He just closed his fist and said something like, "Are you crazy? I am the weakest person in the weakest clan of all Israel? Surely you would know I can't do this." But the angel urged him on. "Don't be afraid." Finally Gideon unlocked the fear in his closed fist but was still a little hesitant and said, "Give me a sign." With the help of the Lord, Gideon **did** lead the Israelites to their freedom.

Remember Mary--that shy young girl just betrothed to Joseph? She must have treasured her dreams of the future, till IT happened. Mary surely clutched both hands in fear, when the angel suddenly appeared from nowhere. Try to imagine it. This teenage girl confronted by an angel. Then, to make things even worse, he said, "Don't be afraid, Mary. You are to have a Son who shall be called Jesus. He will be the Son of God."

A lot of discussion followed with Mary giving reasons why this couldn't happen while the angel assured her that it could. In the end, Mary opened her fearful hands to the Lord saying, "Behold, I am the handmaiden of the Lord." And she became the mother of our Lord and Savior, Jesus Christ.

We must look at just one more. I'm sure Paul would be very indignant if we left him out. Saul (Paul's beginning name) was a one-man demolition team against the Christians. He sought them out in every corner of the country. He was on his way to Damascus, clenching his hands into fists as he thought of all those evil Christians he would expose and bring to prosecution.

Suddenly he was struck down on the road--totally blinded. You may know the story. It was only after he was taken to Ananias that the change came. There he regained his sight, spread out his clenched hands to be touched by God, and became Paul, the evangelist of the ages. Truly, don't many of us look to him as the father of our beliefs as he spread the good news of Jesus Christ to the Gentiles throughout the Mediterranean world?

O.K. Pretty good stories. Right? But what do they have to do with you or me or Donna's "broke" butterfly?

I suggested earlier that we all probably have something in life that is *all broke*. Maybe you haven't really thought about it? O.K. then, are you willing to take a look? Close your fist tighter as you read on. Try to imagine what's clutched inside--what brokenness that you would so like to mend.

It could be a relationship with another person or yourself. Maybe something you want to do--a step into the unknown that you would like to take, but fear or something else holds you back. Is a shattered dream held there, or forgiveness that you need to give or receive, or a hurt so deep that nothing eases the pain. Only you and God know what brokenness you are holding in that fist.

Maybe you're thinking, "I don't need to do this. I can fix it myself. I just haven't gotten around to it yet." Time passes, it's still there. Is your hand getting tired? Fingers hurt a little trying to hold on to those "broken wings" that only you and God know are hidden there?

Open your hand. Let God touch that brokenness held there and show you the way to the mending. It happened for Sarah and Gideon and Mary and Paul. It can happen for you. Just open your hand and let God handle it this time, then be willing to go the distance with him.

It's true. Mamas can't fix 'all broke' butterflies, dear Lord, how many times have I wished I could; but it's OK, even better than OK. We have a loving Lord who yearns to fix our brokenness in ways we can't even imagine. It does take some action on our part. It's up to each one of us to open our hand and our heart as we whisper, "Touch me Lord, your will be done."

Then get ready for the ride of your life.

Baked In The Squat

Would you ever believe that I know very little about baking? I'm the person who never gets a call for baking donations—with good reason.

Even though this is true, I can tell about this unusual title "baked in the squat" because the baking project in this story never ever gets off the bottom of the pan. I can relate to this.

Several years ago I took a couple of students to Houston for a national business students' contest. A very good people motivator Zig Ziglar told us about 'Maude' at one of the seminars.

In Yazoo City, Mississippi there lived a really good cook, Maude. One time Zig was having dinner with the family who employed Maude and she served the guests some silver-dollar thin biscuits. When asked what happened, Maude laughed and said, "Well, these little ole biscuits squatted to rise, but they fooled around so long they got baked in the squat." Everyone joined Maude in the laughter.

On the flight home, I thought about Maude and those silver-dollar thin biscuits. Did you ever know someone who was a little like those biscuits? Someone who's gonna' do something when the time is right. Maybe when summer comes or when summer is over? When the kids get out of school? Or go back to school?

Or maybe you know someone who has "half-a-mind" to do something. Half-a-mind to take a class or maybe teach a class. Half-a-mind to take a trip or stay at home. Or half-a-mind to get more active in church. "Someday I'm going to get around to doing something, but what? Or maybe all of them will just keep on finding excuses and there they are, "baked in the squat."

The Bible is not without individuals who found themselves in this kind of predicament. Do you think it might have all started in the garden—Adam and Eve had paradise, but they didn't rise to the trust God had placed in them. Instead, they followed their own weaknesses and they were banished from Eden, and humanity has been baked in the squat ever since.

Look at Moses. Here's an example of someone who tried REALLY hard not to "rise" to God's expectations, but God didn't give up. Every time Moses came up with a reason for NOT helping the Israelites and leading them out of slavery, God came up with a better reason for moving ahead. In the end, Moses discovered that, with God's help, he could do all the things he thought he couldn't. He faced Pharoah, he faced rebellion; followed a promise and kept on until he finally led the children of Israel to the gates of the promised land.

And didn't he rise!!! And didn't he shine!!!

It was different with the people of Nazareth. They had MORE than half-a-mind to doubt the words of Jesus as He spoke in the synagogue. After all—who did this Jesus think He was? What experience did He have to offer? How dare He claim to be fulfilling a prophecy? Wasn't He the son of Joseph, the carpenter? Didn't He live just down the way?

The more they talked, the angrier they became. Finally the "good" people of Nazareth decided to throw Jesus over a cliff to get rid of him. Now that certainly took more than "half-a-mind." But God opened the way and Jesus left Nazareth. And the *good* people of Nazareth missed a chance to rise and shine.—to reach out and know the long-promised Messiah—so close, yet so far away.

There are so many others who missed their chance on that road from Nazareth to Jerusalem. The foolish Pharisees who were so tied up on the details of the law, that they missed the joy of living. The Samaritan village that refused to let Jesus come in, so they never knew the gift of life he had to offer. Who can forget the ten maidens who were invited to the wedding feast—five slept and let their lamps burn low while they were waiting. Five were prepared for the long wait. The moment came—the five who were ready rose up and entered the joyous festivities. The tragic five who were unprepared were left out in the darkness—baked in the squat.

Perhaps the most poignant figure of all is the rich young man who had "half-a-mind" to follow Jesus—he lived by the law, surely he loved his neighbor—but he went away, sad; when he found out that his wealth would have to take second place to Jesus. His time came, then passed him by. You got it. He was baked in the squat.

Some times the lazy days of summer find us kind of sitting on the bottom of the pan. We know autumn is coming, and that will be a "rising time" so we take it easy. But maybe it's a good time to take a look at where we are with our baking skills. Just where are you in your journey as a child of God. Is it possible that you are stuck in the oven with half-a-mind?

Look inward. What do you see there? Paul once reminded the Ephesians that "God has made us what we are and in our union with Christ Jesus, he has created us for a life of good deeds." In another place Jesus says, "You are the light of the world."

Created for a life of good deeds! The light of the world! Pretty lofty goals, but there is hope for us. We are not biscuits, rather we are children of a living God, created in his image, and we need only to search carefully and diligently for that light he wants us to be. We must be ready, ready to rise, ready to shine.

Several years ago I spent a couple of summers with some American Indian friends who did a lot of traveling. We went to some really neat places but there was one problem. We never knew when Papa Rice was going to come in and say, "Let's go." In a few minutes everyone who was ready would be in the cars and on the road. After being left behind a few times, I learned a very valuable lesson—If you wanted to go everytime, you had to stay packed..

If you're going to live your life with fullness and meaning, you have to stay packed—be ready to grasp the light shining on good deed opportunities that come your way. Sometimes it's something that's been carefully planned that offers these moments. More often than not it's the unexpected times along the daily pathway. Times like giving a word of encouragement or cheer, sharing a smile or a tear, making a call, writing a letter, listening—just listening.

When I was teaching one winter, a few teenagers let their light shine and it warmed me in such a way. My sister's husband had been desperately ill and it had been heavily on my mind. My patience had been short and I had been less than sympathetic to my students' needs. Finally one day I decided to share with them a bit of what I'd been feeling. They said very little, but the next day, tucked between the pages of my plan book, I found a card signed by all of them. In essence it said, "God cares for you and so do we. Hang in there, Mrs. D." Those students did some rising and shining and in doing so, they lifted me up.

It does take something extra to rise. For buttermilk biscuits, I think it's the "pinch of sodie." Maybe it's bakin' powder, but it's something.

The same is true for us. If we are going to rise, it's that pinch of something inside that counts. Jesus promises us over and over that we will have the presence of the Spirit to help us, to be with us and in us. In his letter to the Colossians, Paul repeats the promise so simply, but so powerfully—the secret is: Christ in you, the hope of glory.

CHRIST in you—yet how often do we feel like Charlie Brown. From the moment Charlie set foot on the stage of life, everyone said, "He's not right for the part," and he believed it.

Do you think you are not "right" for the part? Don't you believe it. There is a part for you in this wonderful life and with CHRIST IN YOU, you ARE right for it.

Stop placing barriers in your way. But you hold back, sighing, "When I'm not afraid, when I'm not embarrassed, when I have the money, or the time, or the energy, or the talent, or the inclination, or who knows what else All of these are barriers to your rising, to being the best that you can be—a child of the King.

Of all the men and women we meet in the pages of the Bible, I believe the one least likely to have been caught "baked in the squat: would have been Paul. We first meet him as a man of action, but all that energy is directed against the Lord. It was only after he's struck blind that he is able to see—to see the light of the Lord.

Then all of his energy and wisdom is redirected to work for the same Lord that he had been persecuting. He became a light—not just for his world, but for ours.

Still, after years of evangelizing and spreading the Good News, Paul wrote from prison, "I have not yet reached mature perfection, but I run straight toward the goal." For Paul, nothing stood in his way and he continued to rise to the calling of his Lord.

Jesus gives us the Good News, "I have come that you might have life, life in all its fullness." What greater gift than this—life in all its fullness.

What does this mean to you? What would be on your list to make a full life? Possessions, good health, travel, friends, fame, power? These sound good. But as you think of your choices, remember the rich young man. What would really make a full life? When I was a little girl, Daddy would show me a dime and a nickel. Which do you want, he would ask. I always chose the nickel because it was bigger. Be careful how you measure true value. Don't go away sad.

Rise and shine. Remember the "silver dollar thin" biscuit? I think maybe we should remember that this biscuit is not totally worthless. If we were hungry, it could help a little.

But what about that beautiful, fluffy biscuit? The one that says Step out in faith, believe and receive. The time is now—today—don't be the one baked in the squat.

Fix It, Jesus

Sometimes just looking through a hymn book can bring an unexpected pleasure, one might find a real treasure. The hymn, Fix It, Jesus, was such a find. It's an old Afro-American Spiritual and I guess it wasn't the song so much as the name that attracted me.

Think of it. Isn't this what I'm looking for as I fumble my way along? As I seek the answers to daily living? Fix it, Jesus? Isn't it what we're all looking for?

I went to the gospels and found endless examples of different seekers coming to Jesus; all looking for a solution to a problem--each one unique to his or her distress. Still each problem seemed to be universal to all people, everywhere, in whatever age.

For more than three years, Jesus and his disciples walked the dusty roads from Capernaum to Jerusalem. During those three years, great crowds of people followed him. They had heard the rumors--there is a man who can do wondrous things. He can help us. He has answers to our problems. He can fix things.

In their sicknesses they came: the paralytic, the blind, the deaf, the lepers, the ones with fevers or demons. With their fears they came: the lost and hungry, those who were in sorrow, and despair and turmoil; and, yes, even those seeking eternal life.

Today, one thing is sure, we're still coming to Jesus, to this man who can do wondrous things. Maybe the problems have different names but they boil down to the same thing. Ease my pain, heal my illness, comfort me in my sorrow, feed me when I'm hungry, help me up the ladder, reward me when I've been *good*, stay with me when I'm afraid, forgive me when I sin, and, as he tells it, even save my soul. Fix it, Jesus!

Maybe you're thinking, "What's wrong with this? Besides it isn't ALWAYS for myself that I'm asking." Well, I'm not suggesting anything is <u>wrong</u>. I'm just saying, "Let's go a little further."

Matthew, Mark, Luke and John tell of any number of eyewitness stories of people encountering Jesus. They tell of the rich man and the thief, the terrified disciples and the official of great faith, the ambitious mother and the hungry crowd. Let's take a closer look.

Dare to step into that little boat with the disciples. After a long day, pushed in all directions by the crowds, a weary Jesus lay down to rest. In the darkness a sudden storm came out of nowhere. As the waves grew higher, the boat rocked dangerously. The terrified disciples looked at one another, then toward the sleeping Jesus. "How can He sleep like that? Doesn't He care about us?" Finally in desperation, they shouted, "Jesus awake, awake! Fix this now!"

How many times have I been there in that same *rocking boat?*" A ringing phone which shatters the quiet night, a child gasping for breath, a car spinning out of control, a doctor whose serious eyes lock with mine--and the gut-wrenching fear grabs me. My mind reaches out in a spontaneous cry, "Dear Jesus, you've got to fix this!"

I know I'm not the only one. All people have been in the rocking boat. Do you think maybe they just didn't know it?

We move on to Bethany, standing with the grieving friends of Mary, sister of Lazarus. She runs ahead and our hearts reach out as she falls at the feet of Jesus, "Why did my brother have to die?" she weeps. "Why, Lord? You could have fixed it."

I think of the times I too have wept at His feet with sorrow flooding my soul and tears spilling down my face as I demanded to know: Why, Lord? He went too soon. I still needed him. Why didn't you <u>fix it</u>? Or another time I pleaded, "I wasn't ready for this. I relied on her wise counsel. My children loved her so. Why didn't you <u>fix it</u>? And once more, "Lord, I'm asking again, "Why? She was so courageous and surely too young. I really tried to get ready this time, Lord. But I just couldn't; I didn't want to give her up yet. I'm begging to know, "Why didn't you <u>fix it</u>?"

Selfish cries that go on until I am exhausted and finally give myself into the loving arms of Jesus and realize that he does <u>fix it</u>. He always carries me through the winter to the joy of another springtime. And I am reassured as I remember His words--Everyone who lives and believes in me will never die.

Surely, you too, have been in this same valley of the shadow. And have you found the peace of his loving arms?

Let's return to the crowd and watch the rich, young man go to Jesus. He had everything--youth, wealth, status--what could he possibly want Jesus to fix? Mark continues with the story--the rich, young man asked for eternal life. Jesus said, "Go, sell all that you have and give it to the poor." We're told the young man went away sad.

Wait a minute. This one is different. This guy was rich. I'm not rich, so how does this story apply to me? But it's not so different, because it's not really the money--it's what the money represents. It was something that came first with the man, it stood between him and Jesus. So we're told that he went away sad. I've always wondered about that. Was he sad because he couldn't give away the money or because he was giving up eternal life or both?

What stands between you and Jesus, or me and Jesus; because at one time or another, there is something. We must identify the problem and then do something about it--easy enough for me to say. No, it's not easy, but we're not without help.

After the rich man left, the disciples were confused with 'the fix.' They turned to Jesus, "If this is the way to eternal life, how can anyone be saved?" "No one can do this alone," replied Jesus, "but with God, all things are possible."

We continue to go along with Jesus through the long days on the dusty road as he meets people coming to Him again and again, with the same plea, "Fix it, Jesus." He stretches out his hands in compassion and often gives them what they seek. But many times there is a touch of sadness in the giving, because He has so much more to give. They asked for a drink of water to quench a physical thirst--Jesus had the gift of living water to quench the distress of the soul and give eternal life.

When our children were little and the 'wheels came off the wagon,' everything was all broken, they would take the toy or the problem to their father, "Daddy, fix it!" Because he loved them, he would put things back together for them.

Of course, John usually had to try for himself first. But aren't we all a little like that. We think we can fix our own 'wheels off' problems.

Jesus said, "Except that you become as a child. . ."

With you and with me, we must use the strength of faith to become as a child, His child--and with implicit trust in the promises, we must look to Jesus. And in his eyes, in fear, we find peace--in pain, we find ease--in sorrow, we find comfort, and in dying, we find eternal life.

"Jesus, fix me." Sounds like a gimmick? A little trite? But it's not. These pleadings come from the depths of the soul. They pour out from the humanness of God's creation. They are <u>real</u> and the answers are <u>real</u>.

And so we have it--Jesus really did hang on that cross; in agony, He really died; in glorious victory, He rose and walks among us and leaves with us the continuing promise of hope and joy--I will be with you always. Believe it!

And you know, He walks with me, I do believe, and that's 'fix enough' for me!

Love Spoken Here

Love! How do you say it? *Amore, lieben, tyibva, tea mo, agape*! A word spoken around the world. The language may be different but the meaning is the same. Like the wind, we feel it, but we can't see it. We write stories and poems about it, sing songs about it and even paint pictures of how we think love 'looks.'

But what is it really? What is love? Can it be that the truth may be that it is beyond any simple description.

Jesus put it at the heart of the greatest commandment: Love the Lord your God with all your heart and all your soul and all your mind; then He added a second commandment, love your neighbor as you love yourself.

And so we do! Or do we? We meet together and proclaim our love of God. We love our families, our friends and it seems fairly easy— wonderful, warm and comforting. And we say: YES! Love is the language spoken here.

But Jesus said something else in Luke 6:32. "If you love only the people who love you, why should you receive a blessing? Even sinners love those who love them." Then it gets even tougher. In Luke 6:35 He says, "Love your enemies and do good to them . . . expect nothing back." What? Expect nothing????????

Suddenly we find that love becomes a very risky business. As we share our lives and the love flows outward, we feel good. We wait for that love that's sure to flow inward. But it doesn't always happen and as we open ourselves to others, we become very vulnerable; and hurt may come with the expectations of a return.

Jesus understands this kind of hurt, for when he brought perfect love to this imperfect world, he was rejected. Yet in the face of that rejection, he said, "The greatest love a person can have for his friends is to give his life for them." He said it—then, he **did** it. He gave his life for his friends—and for his enemies, for the world—for you and me; and even as He hung on that cross, dying, he prayed, "Father, forgive them." Forgive the very ones who hung him there? It was true **then**; it's true **today**.

Surely this is too much. Our limited human understanding can scarcely get beyond the fringes of this kind of love.

The depth of our ability to love is related directly to the depth of our faith Do we have the faith to empty our hearts of resentment and bitterness toward family members, friends, coworkers, even enemies who have disappointed us in some way, who have hurt us, perhaps even betrayed us? Can we reach out to them in love and forgiveness? Can we say in the peace that is promised to follow? Yes, love is spoken here.

I mentioned that love is risky. Some years ago when I first began teaching, I decided I should have a puppy. I listened to all the reasons why I shouldn't have one, but I had found one and I wanted her. I lived alone and Taffy received all my attention, when I had the time that is. As a new teacher, I was kept very busy; but it was great having a puppy to pet and cuddle, to sit nearby while I graded papers in the evening. I could talk to her and got no 'back talk.'

One morning when she was about six months old, she woke me and wanted out. "Oh Taffy, it's too early. I'm so sleepy." But I knew I'd be sorry if she didn't go out. Then I made a very unwise decision, "She's old enough to go out by herself." There were no fences and a highway just down the drive. I let her out anyway and went back to bed.

Later, I answered a knock at my door. My school superintendent stood there with Taffy's collar. "I'm sorry, Mildred, I found her on the highway. I took care of it, but I thought you would want her collar."

With tears, I thanked him. As I sat turning the collar over and over and crying, I kept asking myself the age-old question--why? I should have listened to everyone. I shouldn't have bought the puppy. But I knew that was not the answer. I had taken the risk of love, and though she was gone now, it had been worth it. I still remember that puppy with a warmth in my heart.

So I would ask you now—don't choose to walk the way of darkness. With each sun's rising, make a new resolve to say, "Lord, I welcome your love commandments. I embrace every word. I choose to accept the risk. Whether the day's path be one of sadness or one of joy, I walk with sure feet because with all of my heart and all of my soul and all of my mind, I choose to walk with your kind of love."

Could it be that some day, in a language understood by all the world, we could say, "Welcome! Love is spoken here."

Not For Sale

My Great Aunt Jessie was a farmer's wife in Central Illinois. When it came time, her funeral service was much like her life—very unpretentious. There was no listing of great deeds, no statues of her image were erected in the vegetable garden, her name wasn't recorded for posterity in any books and her material wealth certainly didn't cause a stir. A side note--Aunt Jessie's father was Christian Murphy, my great grandfather, who built the Salem Church of God in a cornfield only a couple of miles from Aunt Jessie's farmstead.

Those few friends and family who came to that little country church in the pine trees to remember Jessie, heard the minister sum up her whole life with these words: Throughout her 87 years, Jessie touched many lives around her with a quiet simplicity. She found favor with God.

On the other hand, let's look at another woman. Mother Teresa was a missionary in India. Of course, you know of her and her great works. From far away in Calcutta, she touched the world—her life was one of reaching out to people—the suffering and the dying, the lonely, the poor, the hungry, and countless others of all ages. Throughout <u>her</u> 87 years, as this tiny lady tended to others with a quiet simplicity, she always followed her philosophy, "The good news is that God loves us. Let us be grateful for that love by loving others." She found favor with God.

Two *good* women living totally different lives thousands of miles apart on opposite sides of the world, yet a common thread ran through both their lives. Both found "favor" with God—because they earned it! Right? NO! NO! NO! Wrong!!!!!

And I say this because? Why?

Let's take a look at the nature of God's favor. Throughout the Bible in both the old and new testaments, I found the words "favor" and "grace" somewhat interchangeable. Some say that the doctrine of God's grace is really hard to grasp. Hundreds, maybe thousands, of books and papers have been written to explain this theological concept. This seemed a little too deep for me, so I did my own exploration for understanding.

Grace! What does that mean to you? How would you explain it? Maybe it just has to shine through your life as you live it and as others see it!

I began my search in an old Bible dictionary and found these words--grace, the 'kindness' of God toward the human race.

Kindness. Hm-m-m. Is that too mild for such a significant word? I searched a little further for kindness and found that "an act of kindness is an act of truly giving. It is an outpouring of feeling with little thought of return." OK, that's not too tough, but I wanted to know a little more. In his book Systematic Theology, Alva Huffer writes, "The Greek word for grace is *charis*—kindness given freely without consideration of merit or recompense."

Finally, I turned to some of the new testament writings and there was John the Baptist, walking the dusty roads of Judea. He was telling the people, "You had better get ready, the 'light' is coming." Of course, he meant Jesus, the Savior. John went on to say, "He is the one greater than I. God gave the Law through Moses, but grace and truth came through Jesus Christ." Grace and truth!!!!!

After being in the desert for 40 days and dealing with all the devil's temptations, Jesus made his way to the Jordan River. There was that same John who had predicted the 'light' was coming. Jesus presented himself for baptism. At first John refused. I would imagine that in his heart perhaps John felt unworthy to baptize Jesus, even if He was a relative, he knew Him to be the promised Savior. But Jesus persisted and John led him into the water. Afterward, the spirit of God came down as a dove and God said, "This is my beloved Son with whom I am well-pleased."

Grace from God, through Jesus Christ. Was there still more to know?

Perhaps no one told us more about the grace of God than the apostle

Paul. Actually in his letters to the churches of the New Testament, Paul mentions "the grace of God" over a hundred times. Perhaps nowhere more poignantly than in 2 Corinthians 12:9. In his persistent way, three times Paul had asked God to take away the painful physical condition that plagued him. But three times God's answer was, "My grace is sufficient for your need." God went on to say, "My power is greatest when you are weak." Now Paul, being Paul, was able to accept that answer and praised God. Can we do that? Can we praise God when he doesn't see things our way?

Sometimes I find myself confronted with something tough (at least I think it is) and like Paul, I go to the Lord—"It's too much. Take it away." Sometimes, again just like Paul, the answer seems to be, "My grace is sufficient, deal with it." But there the comparison stops. I may find myself thinking—whoa! wait a minute. Look, Lord, I've been trying to deal with this, but I can't. I want this problem gone--NOW.

Finally, after spinning like a hamster on a treadmill, I think more about that "sufficient" grace and what it means. The way seems to open up a little or even a lot when I'm ready to yield to His leading. And I find myself praying, "Forgive me, Lord, looks like my faith was a little shaky there for a while. I guess I put your gift of grace over there in a dark corner. Please help me to rethink the problem."

Think of times in your own life when you've hit the wall, till finally battered and bruised, with God's leading and your yielding, you find the way over or under or around the bricks. Once more, His grace is sufficient when you completely turn it over to God. (Did I say this is easy?)

Let's go back for a minute to the baptism of Jesus. Remember what the spirit of God said? "This is my beloved Son with whom I am pleased!"

Why wouldn't God be pleased, that was Jesus standing there in the Jordan. And from there He was ready to go to the desert for 40 days of testing by Satan. And His answer to all of the temptations? "Go away Satan!" And again I ask, "What about you? What about me?"

I think of times when things go wrong and I'm in the middle of what Mama would call "a real hissy fit." I can just picture a saddened Lord watching from above and saying, "This is my beloved daughter with whom I'm disappointed." Disappointed?????

Of course he's disappointed. At that moment I'm standing a long way from all the promises I made when I accepted Jesus .I am disappointed. This is personal.

It seems to me the operative word is <u>beloved</u>. This is my <u>beloved</u> daughter—cause no matter what, God does love us. We can't earn that love or bargain for it or buy it. It's called "God's grace" and it's <u>not for sale!</u> You won't find it at the bargain barn on the corner or the most exclusive shop in the upscaled mall. It's God's Grace and IT IS FREE!!!!!!

This is probably one of the most difficult concepts to be found in our personal relationships with God. But once we can accept it, we can gain a great freedom to live our lives in wonderful ways.

When I was growing up, there were rules, but I never thought much about them. I knew Daddy loved me and because of the love between us I <u>wanted</u> to do the 'right' thing usually. Did I always? Of course not. Just ask my sister. But when I strayed, after we talked about it together (which for me was worse than a trip to the woodshed) Daddy always forgave me and it was never brought up again. That was my earthly father's grace.

The Bible reminds us that the grace of the heavenly father is so much greater than that of our earthly father. Again we turn to Paul, this time as he writes to the Ephesians—"By grace you have been saved through faith. This is not your own doing. It is a gift of God!"

Another mystery. What have I done to deserve this wonderful gift? Nothing, except to be born a child of God. Just like you.

What greater action of "truly giving" has ever been shown than when Jesus went to the cross for me? This single act was an outpouring of unmatched love that flows in a pure unending stream throughout the universe. In the trials and troubles of life's journey, we face disappointments and joys, sickness and health, poverty and wealth and finally, death. But no matter where we are along the way, we need only dip our cup into that stream of love to quench the pain of confusion and desperation, for it is truly as he promised, "My grace is sufficient."

This grace of God surrounds you as a beautiful garden, with flowers not for sale. They are yours for the picking. We are assured over and over that his grace will fill our needs.

Remember my earlier question, "Did the ladies "earn" the granting of God's favor?" NO! My great aunt Jessie and even Mother Teresa did not "earn" the grace of our Lord by their deeds. Rather, the deeds were the **result** of their accepting the grace so freely offered. As we are reminded from the scripture in Ephesians 2—"God has made us what we are, and in union with Christ Jesus he has created us for a life of good deeds."

I don't know how it is with you, but this I do know about me. I believe with all my heart that Jesus DID go to the cross for me and his incredible presence is with me everywhere, every minute of every day and night..

In the same way, He DID go to the cross for you. As His beloved son or daughter, trust his grace; dip into that river of his "loving kindness" and drink deeply of His blessing. God's gift of amazing grace is ***not for sale***. Why do you hesitate? It's yours for the taking.

So JUST DO IT!

Baked Fresh Daily

Sometimes a little morning stroll along a familiar street offers a bonus. A delicious, tempting aroma drifts on the winds. You start searching for the source 'cause you already know there can be only one thing that smells that good. As you savor another deep breath, the sign says it all, "Bread--baked fresh daily."

There's other places you can find this treat--perhaps in a friend's kitchen. Maybe it's yours. For sure it's not mine, since I'm not a baker, but that doesn't make the aroma any less tantalizing or a thick, warm hunk any less tasty.

It's a little amazing to me how a few simple ingredients: flour and water, a little salt and shortening can produce this delicious staple of life. What! You say I left something out. Of course, the one ingredient that makes it all come together--the yeast. (And here's a thought--punching down the dough and giving it some serious kneading can produce some substantial therapy for frustrations. But slow down, that's a whole other story.)

You can't spend time in the Gospels without discovering that Jesus talks a lot about bread and water and even grain. Feeding the five thousand, the woman at the well, eating at the fire with his disciples, the parables which center around planting and harvesting and eating. These were the everyday ways of living that the people understood. He used all of these to spread his message of hope and help.

Then, as was Jesus' way, he moved beyond the physical. He spoke of the *bread of life* and offered the *living water.*

But times were hard and the Roman rule was rigid. We might wonder,

"How did they do it? How did they meet the daily challenges and keep their faith?"

Do you sometimes wonder about this? Perhaps you question, with me, "How can I keep my faith baked fresh daily?"

There are three central ingredients for this faith loaf that seems to be essential: look inward, reach outward, stretch upward.

Look inward. Search within yourself to discover your special worth. In the whole world. there is no one now nor has there ever been anyone exactly like you. Find an acceptance of who you are, because you are a child of God. Yes, you have all the frailties of being human, but still you are a child of God.

And as one of His, listen to what Jesus has to say about YOU--you are the salt of the earth -- a light for the whole world -- worth more than the birds whom the Father cares for. But here is the bottom line. God loved you so much that He sacrificed his Son for your salvation.

As the poster says, "God don't make junk!" Sometimes we forget this, and we see ourselves tarnished and tattered, but God can polish us up just fine if we only let him. Search within yourself to discover your gifts that are meant to be shared with others. What person or project awaits your special touch? Look inward to discover; then follow God's will for you life.

The second ingredient would be: reach outward. So maybe you're asking, "What am I reaching for?" No, you're not reaching "for," you're reaching "to give." So many ways of giving come to mind. Singing, teaching, talking, praying, cooking, sharing, there's no end to the ways.

There's less obvious ways that are just as vital. Things like a phone call, a flower given, a willing listening ear, a wall to be painted, a nail to be driven, a note of encouragement, a baby to be rocked, a warm meal or maybe, just a loaf of fresh-baked bread. Do these seem too simple? Too easy?

Recently at a time when I was scraping the bottom of the pan, I received a little card from a friend. It had one line printed across a garden of flowers, "God made someone special when he made you." I'm not even sure why she sent the card, or why that day. What I do know because she reached outward, it gentled the storm, and resulted in a better day for those around me.

It seems our churches are in need at this time: For a Martha who will say, "I'll be in the kitchen, for a Mary who says, "You'll find me sitting at Jesus' feet." We need a Peter or a Paul who declares, "I will travel far and wide, even to Rome," and a James who will stay in Jerusalem.

The calls are different and sometimes we attach our own job descriptions to certain calls. The pastor has a special calling toward the pulpit, but sometimes his greatest service can be that continual care he offers: the middle of the night call, the comfort, the guidance, the listening.

How often must the pastor hear these words, "Preacher, I need to talk to you." a crying out when we are so lost and so cold--like sheep in need of that special shepherd, one who can lead us back to the fold.

In one way or another, we are all commissioned to "feed the lambs."

My great aunt was an unassuming little lady, a farmer's wife, the mother of two sons. I remember that she usually wore a flowery dress, covered with a big wrap-around apron. The apron was very often sprinkled with another kind of "flour." She always made the bread for communion Sunday. For her, it was a very special job, her way of reaching outward. She carried herself with a certain calm that also touched others.

I believe she must have looked inward to discover the strength, then as she attempted to follow God's will in the limited world she knew, she reached outward and touched others in a special way. She probably never even thought of her outreach. If anyone would have mentioned it, I think she might have blushed a bit, said "Oh pshaw," and wondered what the person was talking about. I know she touched my life, but I never told her.

Look inward, reach outward, then stretch upward. Just like baking that fresh bread daily, if the first two ingredients are to work, the yeast must be added. We must build a personal relationship with Jesus Christ, and to do this we must first come to know Him.

You can't come to know anyone from a distance. He's not far away. Rather, he's right there at your side, urgently waiting for some sign from you. "Lord, I'd like to get know you. I need you for my friend?"

How can this happen? You've said, "Yes, I believe!" There's no question there. But the problem is the "personal relationship stuff." What can I do? I go to church.

You must make the move! Read about Him, study His words, listen and He will speak to you. The four gospels are filled with the words of Jesus (I like the editions that carry all of Jesus' words in red.) The words may have been spoken first many years ago, but they are alive and relevant for your life today.

Talk with Him. Prayers of course, but talk with Him aloud. If you know the song, "Just A Little Talk With Jesus," sing with Him. If you don't know the song, just "have a little talk." These "little talks" can sort things out--help us put grievances aside, heal hurts, build patience, cool anger, increase tolerance and understanding. Our thinking can be cleared and we are able to see others through eyes of love rather than hate. How desperately our world needs this kind of thinking.

It won't happen in a day. Friendships aren't built in a day, but try it, and I can promise that if you break those walls which separate you from Jesus, the walls which separate you from others will also begin to crumble.

As the years pass, thousands of unassuming men and women, through the grace and guidance of a loving God, have fed the sheep and cared for the lambs from their *faith loaf* baked fresh daily.

"Go forth and do likewise," says our Lord.

Double Dare Ya'

Did you ever play <u>Follow The Leader</u>? My kids did and I certainly did but it might be in trouble as today's favorite game while trying to compete with all the high tech activities.

Our game always began with a line of kids and a leader who started the challenges with fairly easy stuff--a twirling turn around, a leap across a small ditch, swinging off a tree limb, then something a little more difficult like walking a pipeline.

Gradually the leader would become bolder and the kids would start dropping off till only two or three were left. That's when the leader would add, "I dare ya'." Another person would drop out, and the leader shouted, "I double dare ya'!"

We got to know the leaders pretty well, and if I decided it was going to be too tough, I would very conveniently hear my mother calling me to come home to supper.

<u>Follow the leader</u>. Just a kid's game, so what's the connection between this game and a rich young man in the Bible, the one who 'went away sad.' (Have you discovered the rich young man is one of my favorites?)

In both there is a leader and there are followers, but in the story from Matthew, the stakes are so much higher--the dare was to follow Jesus and the prize was eternal life. But the young man was rich and chose to pass.

Maybe it seems strange to think of Jesus in terms of a dare, but when I checked the dictionary, I found this--<u>to dare</u> is to challenge someone to do something hard, to be bold.

Jesus dared the young man to sell everything he had, then to give all the money away. Now I call that a challenge! But the second part seems even more difficult--the part when Jesus said, "Come, follow me." That was the 'double dare' for the rich young man, and for you, and for me.

"Come follow me." I know it's different for each of us. Maybe for some, it's not much of a challenge, but I dare you to take a look at what I think it means 'to follow Jesus' as we move along some of the pathways he traveled.

We join him at a high point, standing in the River Jordon. After some persuasion, John, who has been baptizing people all day, agrees to do the same for Jesus, but with a different ending. A voice is heard saying, "This is my beloved Son. I'm well pleased." Well, I can certainly deal with good things.

But soon we find Jesus in the desert, where he's been meditating and fasting for several days. As He grows weaker, the devil shows up. Knowing he'll never have another chance as good as this, he uses all of his powers of persuasion to try to corrupt this beloved Son of God.

He knows Jesus hasn't eaten for many days, and certainly must be hungry, so he appeals to self-gratification. "If you really are the Son of God, just turn these stones to bread. There's nothing wrong with that. I know you're hungry."

When that doesn't work, he tries coming at him from another direction. (The devil always does.) "Let's see how powerful your God is. Just jump off this high steeple. He'll save you if he really is God. It will be a good test."

Again Jesus refuses. Finally, the devil gives it his best shot--the old power play. "Look down there. All the kingdoms of the world are mine. I'll give them with all their power to you." To all of these temptations, Jesus replied, "Go away, Satan. Do not test the Lord."

I believe Jesus was truly tempted, He could have said yes to Satan. But He didn't. Will I be up to challenges such as these? Will I still be in the game?

After Jesus began his ministry, he traveled up and down the country visiting many towns and villages, always talking with the people--the popular and unpopular, the rich and the poor, the sick and the downtrodden, the wealthy and the powerful.

Let's join him on this very hot day; Jesus is quite weary. Yes, Jesus grew tired, just as all humans do. He stops to rest at a well in Samaria while the disciples go into town for food. Jesus asks for a drink from a woman drawing water. This surprises her. Not only is she a woman, but she is a Samaritan woman. A Jew wouldn't even drink from a cup that a Samaritan had touched. Jesus continues to talk with her. He looks beyond prejudice and differences--she realizes this is someone special. Later, because of her testimony, many of the townspeople went to him to receive the Good News of salvation.

Is it possible for me to get beyond my own prejudice and fear of those who are different? Will I continue to follow the Teacher?

Jesus often went to the temple, but this scene comes most vividly to mind. Here we meet what seems to be a different Jesus. Not only does He take a firm stand against the injustices of the moneychangers, but he does more than talk. He takes action as he overturns the table, scatters the coins and drives the thieves out of the temple area.

Will I be able to accept the dare of standing firm on my beliefs in the face of opposition? Is this where I may be left standing on the sidelines?

"Do not judge others, take the log out of your own eye, then you can see the speck in your brother's eye." Jesus spoke often of the danger of making judgments about others, but never more forcefully than when the Pharisees confronted him with the woman caught in adultery. By the law of Moses, punishment must be sure and swift--stone her! But these guys were trying to trick Jesus, so they put the question to him, "What are we to do with her?" Jesus said, "Let the one who is without sin cast the first stone." I'm sure you know how many stones were thrown that day.

So-o-o, this following is getting harder and harder. (Listen. My mother may be calling me home for supper.) Seriously, how can I look at others without making judgments, especially when I KNOW they are wrong?

These glimpses of the earthly journey of Jesus which began in Bethlehem leads finally to the garden of Gethsemane, where we find him on his knees in great anguish. "Father, my Father, all things are possible for you. Take this cup of suffering away from me." Then He added the *bottom line*, "If it be your will."

We know the 'cup' wasn't taken away because within hours, Jesus was nailed to a cross, where he cried out again, "My God, my God, why have you abandoned me?" Then He died.

Many of those to whom he had said, "Follow me," watched in horror and disbelief, then they ran away.

Dear Lord, this is getting very serious. My childhood game was never like this. Do you really expect <u>me</u> to do more than your own disciples? To stand firm at the cross?

But, of course it's true. You know it and I know it. Jesus is still the leader and he still calls out the dare today--follow me.

And I have, I have followed. I've stood in that desert of temptation. And what happened? I gave in to the passing pleasure of self-gratification. I've tried to test God--if you will just do this one thing for me, then I promise I will do this for you. Let's make a deal. And dear Lord, how many times have I been lured by the siren's song of the power game. Yes, I do follow, but how many times do I stumble and except for your strong arms, I would certainly fall.

So many times I've stopped at the well of tolerance. I talk to people who are different. I make moves toward friendship, sometimes.

And what about standing up. I can stand on the temple steps and shout with the best of them. I'm good at the 'getting angry' part, but I wonder if that's the same thing as speaking out about believing in you?

I can follow you to the garden for praying. "Take this cup away, make things better, don't abandon me, Lord, please, just don't abandon me."

What about it, Lord, I've followed you almost everywhere. But could it be I've had this a little mixed up. To follow you is not just to go to the desert, or the well, or the temple, or the garden or even to the cross. If we dare to live at all, we will find ourselves in these places at one time or another.

But maybe to follow Jesus, to really follow him, is to accept the challenge of what we <u>do</u> in these places. Can I resist evil temptation with all the strength of my being? Can I reach out in love and compassion to all that cross my path, or the ones I may look for?

Can I leave no doubt about my convictions for the Lord, no matter on what steps I may stand. Can I accept the challenge to view others with understanding and leave the judging to the Lord? And when I truly must, can I pray, "Let the cup pass, but let me accept your will, no matter what."

Can I be thankful in all things and know, truly know, that God will work for my good if I but seek his plan for my life? I know I_can, Lord, you proved that, but the question is, will I?

I ask with the disciples, "This is hard, who, Lord, can be saved?" And the Lord replies, "It's not possible--not with man, but with God, all things are possible."

In our journey with Jesus, we left him on the cross. But that wasn't the end. With the Easter sunrise, Jesus returned to once again give the challenge--follow me.

Faith is trusting God to direct our daily walk and be with us in all things. With this kind of trust, it is possible to risk the dare to follow Jesus, to truly put him first in our lives and be assured that we can stay in the game all the way.

I know I want to be in this game to stay. I dare ya' to follow Him. No. This is worth more than a dare. I double dare ya'.

PART THREE

—

Special People

His Name *Shalt* Be Called JESUS!

And the angel said to Mary, "Thou shalt call His name Jesus."
Greek Diaglott Translation By Benjamin Wilson Luke 1:31b

Jesus...It seems such a simple name after all those tongue twisters in the old Testament.

Jesus...a name to be sung from the trusting child's "Jesus Loves Me" to the mid-years of "Jesus Calls Me", till we stand at the gates of life eternal, "Precious Lord, Take My Hand."

Jesus...His name calls to us in the very presence of all life.

He calls to me in the presence of my joy--the miracle of the birth of my children, the continual renewal of my marriage, the gift of a friend's loving support, a moment of remembrance shared with an aging parent and Jesus says, "Rejoice, my child, these are times to be treasured. Sit with Me for a bit."

He calls to me in the presence of my grief--a great, crushing grief that fills every crevice of my soul as I face yet another farewell of a loved one, and cry out in pain, "Why? Why?" and Jesus says, "Hush my child, I, too, have been in this garden. Lean on Me."

He calls to me in the presence of my despair as I wander in a night black with loneliness, searching, ever searching--Where am I? Where am I going? Who am I? and Jesus says, "Hush, hush, you are God's child and loved beyond all understanding. Rest here with Me awhile."

He calls to me in the presence of the earth's beauty--the sky, the sweep of the ocean, the majesty of the mountains and the warmth of the sun till I am overcome by my lack of worthiness to receive these precious gifts and

Jesus says, "Hush, my child, do you not remember that it is pleasing to God to give these gifts to you?"

Jesus--Yes, it IS more than a name for as we reach out a trembling hand to touch the man, Jesus, we touch the face of **God**.-----------------

Best-est Friends Forever

Who's your best friend? Your best-est friend? (Actually my computer is telling me with a little squiggly red line that there is no *best-est* friend.) Well that just goes to show you that computers don't know everything.

When children are young, they seem to be content to have a couple of other children playing nearby and as long as one doesn't try to snatch away a toy from the other, there's usually not a problem. Today, parents schedule something called "play dates" and a time and place is worked out for the kids to get together for play. I'm sure my mama never scheduled a "play date." She just sent us outside, and before you knew it, several kids had shown up to play. (As a mother, I don't remember scheduling play dates either.) I'm not saying this doesn't work well in today's busy schedule.

From sandpiles to sleepovers, best friends seem to steadily rise in importance. I wonder if I could have survived the traumas of junior high and high school without my best friend. We shared secrets and sandwiches, giggles and tears, sweaters and sunburns--and it wasn't always with the same best friend. For whatever reasons, sometimes a friendship seemed to slip away, while another would fall into place.

Each year, as a teacher, I would listen to the seniors promise with great emotion, "We'll be best friends always and see each other all the time." Of course, it rarely happens that way and many of these friendships go the way of graduation tassels--treasured memories, but rarely touched.

Once in a great while, a rare and special friendship comes along. It blooms in beauty for a time--then is preserved in gold. For me, such a friendship came to be. It began in our college days; then, of course, we went our separate ways. Today, we are separated by many miles, still, I think of her often. I know she thinks of me and because of this, when we have that once-a-year meeting, the words flow non-stop--we laugh, may even cry a little, and for a few hours it is as it was--and Bonnie and I are together.

James and I have lived in several different places and sometimes someone will say, "How can you do it, leave every one behind and start finding friends all over again?" It <u>is</u> hard to leave the security of good friends behind; but I've found that every new place has the seeds of new friendships waiting to grow and bloom. We just need to cultivate them a little.

So many friendships have been woven into the scriptures. Remember Jonathon who risked his position with his father to protect his friend David? I Samuel 20 Another famous old testament story is the loving friendship between Ruth and her mother-in-law Naomi, which has inspired poets throughout the ages. Ruth 1

The disciples tell so many touching stories of Jesus as he deals with His friends. These may serve as guidelines for our friendships.

A FRIEND GRIEVES IN OUR GRIEF John 11:32-35
Lazarus was dead! When Mary met Jesus coming on the road, she was in great sorrow. The people around were weeping and His heart was touched, He was deeply moved and He wept. What comfort this should bring us. As we worry about our need to "bear up", don't let others know your feelings, keep it in, be brave--in the face of all this, Jesus wept.

A FRIEND SHOWS COMPASSION Luke 13:34
Jesus grieved for the people, "Oh, Jerusalem, Jerusalem. You kill the prophets, you stone the messengers. How many times I wanted to put my arms around your people as a hen gathers her chicks under her wings, but you would not let me." How often do I seem to be a part of that flock that runs all over the place, trying to find my own safe spot rather than seek the shelter of His arms?

A FRIEND QUIETS OUR FEAR Matthew 10:31
Jesus said, "I tell you my friends, do not be afraid, for not one sparrow is forgotten by God. Again, do not be afraid, you are worth much more than many sparrows." All of us have those fears, named and unnamed, that creep into our sleepless midnights and we lie there--frightened, alone. But, we don't have to be alone. He offers a healing light for the dark night.

A FRIEND GIVES US PEACE John 14:27
Jesus said, "Peace is what I leave with you; it is my own peace that I give you. Do not be worried and upset; do not be afraid." Some of my days are so mixed up that I begin to wonder if I have somehow flipped over and am walking around on my head. Do you have days like that? Jesus doesn't promise he'll wipe out the turmoil around us, but it's possible, through him, to find the eye of peace within the hurricane. Then we can hang on until the storm passes.

A FRIEND HANGS IN THERE Matthew 28-20b
Jesus promised, "And lo, I will be with you always, to the end of the age." My grandmother always said, "A good friend sticks with you through thick and thin." I used to wonder exactly what "thick and thin" meant, but I never had to question the "sticks" part. That meant the friend could be counted on all the time.

A FRIEND SHARES OUR JOY John 15:11
Jesus said ". . .my joy may be in you that your joy may be complete." What can be more heartwarming than the sharing of joys between friends?

A FRIEND GIVES OF HIMSELF John 6:35, John 15:13
Jesus told the people, "I am the bread of life. He who comes to me will never be hungry, he who believes in me will never be thirsty." "The greatest love a person can have for his friends is to give his life for them." Now that's **really** hanging tough, but that's exactly what Jesus did, and because He gave his life for each of us, we can

be certain He's the dearest friend that we will ever have. He fills all the requirements, He grieves with us, shows compassion, quiets our fears, gives peace, rejoices with us, hangs in there and gives and gives and gives . . . Jesus does all this and more.

Are you looking for a friend? And do you wonder what He requires of His friends?

Only that we believe. The key comes from I John 4:7 "Dear friends, let us love one another because love comes from God. Whoever loves is a child of God and knows God."

I have known and loved many treasured friends over the years. I hope there will be more, but as you read this, if I would truly be your friend, I would say to you, "I'd like you to know my friend, Jesus. Only open your heart to him and you will find the living water flowing. He will give you blessings beyond your dreams. He can make your life sweeter with your family, your friends, with your co-workers, with everyone you touch. Only believe; you will find his love to be truly a blessing that binds."

I know it works this way for me. Won't you let him be your friend, too?

Way To Go, Buddy!

The old man's sat so still? Was he asleep, or was he awake--but dreaming, lost in the lazy haze of an Indian Summer breeze? His eyes were mere slits against the brilliance of the afternoon sun, he seemed completely unaware of the little boy sitting in the leaves nearby.

Was the old man lost in the thought of other days in other places? Was he striding down some long-ago path leading to another dream?

The little boy scooped up some dry leaves, squeezed them between his fingers, then laughed as he opened his hands and the wind caught the crunchy, brown pieces sifting away. He reached out to catch a yellow boat floating by, looked it over very carefully, then let it sail away for other shores.

After awhile he looked up at the old man, who didn't move or make any sign that the child was there. He clapped his hands together as if to shout, "Look at me! Look at me!" Again there was no response; this time the little boy tried to stand--bottom up, hands and feet down. He soon discovered that this method didn't work too well because he tumbled flat and rolled over with a very surprised look on his face.

Still, the old man appeared to see nothing except his own inward panorama.

The little boy tried again. He pushed and pushed, only to fall again, this time on his head. He started to laugh but his little lips turned into a trembling pucker.

The old man's eyes flickered a bit, but nothing else moved. The scene played over again and again, with a few tears added. And I wondered, "What can you be thinking, old man, as you sit there watching this little guy trying so hard. Don't you care? Why don't you help him? I'll help him." Then, so softly that I wondered if it were only the breeze stirring those last leaves of the season, "You can make it, Buddy."

And "make it" he did! With great determination, he planted his sturdy little legs, finally took his hands off the ground and, with a wobbly effort, he stood. He was delighted with himself.

The old man's eyes softened as he reached out a gnarled hand to hold the dimpled one stretching forward. A span of years touching--and in those years the old man found a "fine pearl"--*sometimes he helps best who only stays nearby, lets the growth happen, then cheers!* Way to go, Buddy! Way to go, old man!

The Touch Of The Potter's Hand

One plus of our travels is discovering special places and special people. One surprise was the glassblower who was working his magic in the Craftsmen's Alley at Silver Dollar City. He was just ready to begin as we joined the other travelers gathered around.

The young man opened the fiery oven, chose a long, thin pipe and dipped it into the boiling mass. He carefully removed the pipe and there was a "blob" attached to the end. As he rolled and swung the pipe in all directions, he talked about the wonders of glass. The blob took on a lavender tint as it began to cool. Then putting the pipe to his lips, the real magic began. The blob began to change and grow, leaning first one way and then the other.

Several times he put the creation back into the oven, then out again. Finally a beautiful vase took shape before our eyes. Then disaster! As he took his breathtaking piece from the fire, it grazed the edge of the oven and one side just collapsed. "Oh, no," all the people gasped. The beautiful vase was ruined and the glassblower would surely have to throw it back into the bubbling pot only to become a part of the boiling mass again.

The young man just laughed at our fears. "It's OK," he said. "Sometimes things don't turn out the way I plan, but I can save this. I'll just turn it into a pitcher-vase." He formed a handle and carefully attached it to the cooling 'damaged' vase. Next he did a little work on the other side forming a graceful spout. Finally, there it was--different from the others on the shelf, but really no less beautiful.

Over the years I've often thought about that day and the smashed vase.

There's a familiar time in the Bible (Matthew 7:7-11) which became a great teaching event. Jesus had just called the first four disciples and a large crowd had gathered. I'm thinking as Jesus went up the hill to sit down, it must have been something like an all day service with dinner on the ground.

His words presented many new ideas, especially the teaching on the relationship between people and God and His children. These were revolutionary thoughts--"Ask and it will be given to you; seek, and you will find; knock and the door will be opened to you. For everyone who asks receives; he who seeks finds; and to him who knocks, the door will be opened. . . . Your Father in heaven will give good gifts to those who ask him." Matt 7:7,8,11b.

Now doesn't that sound like something we could certainly believe in? Think about it--ask, seek, knock and it's yours.

Do you think we need to think about this a bit more? Do we read only two verses in the Bible and then close the book on the learning?

We are told over and over again that God wants only the very best for His children and He has a plan for each of us. We are also assured that God's grace will sustain us in this plan. Now here's the bottom line of the matter--we need to actively seek to discover what His plan might be. One sure way is through prayer. Again, we are promised over and over that God answers prayer. Surely all people who know God would agree with that.

Between my Great Aunt Lizzie and Daddy's guidance, I've always been fairly comfortable talking with God. Truthfully, early on, I did find God a little scary, so usually I did my talking with Jesus. But here's the thing. Have you ever found His answer to be NO?

I know I have more than once, and that "NO" answer doesn't sit too well with me. You see, one of my problems was **and is**, that I don't always quite agree with God's plan for my life.

The first big stunning NO! came during my sixteenth summer. It had been a special time. A couple of girls from Kansas had come to Oklahoma to visit their aunt, and when it came time for them to go home, they invited me to come with them for a visit. Now, I REALLY, REALLY wanted to go and since it was important to me, I prayed my hardest that it would happen. I couldn't believe it when God said NO! Of course, He used Mama and Daddy to say the words. I cried and pouted for a whole day after the girls left; then the very next day the unexpected happened. World War II ended, gas rationing was lifted, Daddy's vacation began and he decided the tires would make it to Illinois. Because of the war, it had been four years since we'd been there, and I would have missed it all if I had gone to Kansas.

Now to you, this may seem a silly little thing, but I know as soon as I saw my grandma and aunts and uncles and cousins, I was so thankful for that NO answer to my prayer. Not important! Who decides?

Another NO came many, many years later. (I'm not suggesting there weren't many others in between.) When James had the stroke 25 years ago, there were prayer chains across the country praying for him--first that he would live, then that he would gain some healing and recovery. James remembers that the first two people who came to visit him at the Rehab Center were a couple of guys from our church. I'm sure they were stunned by the appearance of that wreck of a man lying in the bed. But, as time passed, they, along with the rest of us, watched the healing as he moved that first toe a little and finally walked again. No question, God's power through faithful prayers was in evidence.

But I wasn't quite satisfied and as Easter approached, I began to bargain with God. If you can do this God, and I know you can, I want an Easter morning miracle. Just make James' arm move a little. Besides think how great it would look. I know it can happen." Can you believe my audacity? I prayed every day through advent. I didn't tell anyone as I waited for Easter morning.

When we went to church that morning, I watched, ready for the miracle. Gradually, as the arm remained at his side, I realized that movement wasn't going to happen. God's answer was "NO."

I was forced to take a long look at myself. I wondered, "Was my faith not strong enough? Why is the answer NO? Where did I go wrong? Was I putting myself above God's plan with these demands? Was I looking for a little *glory* for myself?"

Honestly, I don't know the answer to these questions, but I think I did finally learn one thing. All my life on some occasions, I tried to bargain with God. Now, I believe there's a better way to pray. God doesn't need my feeble bargains--he wants my love, and footsteps that follow his leading. I'm working on that.

God hasn't hesitated to say "No" to me several times, as I've come up with some pretty ridiculous askings. Not too surprising, but I do believe if it seems important to me, then it's important to talk with God about ALL things.

Let me share just one more experience. When my daughter-in-law Betty was first diagnosed with ovarian cancer, we all prayed for recovery. And it happened--a few times, because the hateful disease would go away, then return. Her life was very rewarding throughout the well times. She entered nurse's training, and after finishing, worked as a nurse in the ICU area in Birmingham. After about six years, it was obvious that the cancer wasn't going away this time. We kept praying for recovery, but this time God was saying "NO."

But, why? "She's so young, only 42. She's a 'good' person. She loves you, God. Aren't these good reasons why she should be with us longer?" But as the end came closer, I began to realize the prayer to keep her was a selfish prayer for our own grief. She was in pain; we had to let her go. It was only later that I came to realize, God's "NO" to us was a "YES" to Betty. Her doctor wrote a letter to Rick which said it all, "Now, she's in a so much better place."

Think of the no's God has sent your way. Have they made you resentful or have they been a pathway toward growing in God's love? In the Bible we can find so many, many times when God dealt with His people with a resounding NO.

We join Moses as he tends the sheep. It all started with that burning bush that didn't burn. God said, "I need you to go back to Egypt and lead the Israelites home. But Moses said, "I'm nobody, I can't go to the king. The Israelites won't believe me. They won't follow me. They'll say you didn't appear to me. I'm not a good speaker." Finally Moses simply said, "No, Lord, please send someone else."

But God had answers for all six excuses--six NO's to Moses. Finally,

Moses could no longer resist Him. And from there, the nation of Israel began again.

Perhaps the greatest NO of all happened in the Garden of Gethsemane. Three times a very human Jesus prayed the agonizing words, "God, spare me from the cross. If it is possible, deliver me from death." But as the blood dripped from his brow, always he added these words, "If it be your will." Then God said NO, for it was his plan through the sacrifice of His Son to give the gift of salvation to all His children.

Ask, seek, knock. But in the asking and the seeking and the knocking, let God be God. Don't limit his power. In His loving grace, God does answer our prayers. But we must keep in mind that sometimes the greatest love is shown in the No answer. It is God's truest, deepest hope that we will choose His way. It takes only that mustard seed faith and nothing will be impossible with you. **These are the words of our Lord, Jesus.**

Remember the pitcher-vase made by the glassblower. As we live our lives, we all would like to be the beautiful, perfect vase filled with fragrant flowers. But sometimes our lives become flattened on one side, or even both sides--ruined, we think. But it doesn't have to be.

With a willingness on our part and help from the Master Craftsman, our ruined life can be reworked. We can get a handle on it and the pitcher we become can be just what God wanted us to be. We need only to say with humble acceptance, "Take my life and let it be."

The Ole Goat Man

"The Gobble-uns 'll git you ef you don't watch out!"
(James Whitcomb Riley)

It wasn't Orphant Annie's gobble-uns that worried us kids who lived on the Sinclair Plant 12 lease near Seminole OK. No matter what kind of trouble we managed to find, all Mamas would shake a finger and promise in hushed tones, "That Ole Goatman'll git you if you don't watch out!"

From the day our family moved into our shotgun house, there were whisperings about the Ole Goatman. Often on summer evenings after supper, the kids would gather in the deepening twilight for story time.

As the heat of the summer day dropped with the sun and the whipping wind became a softer breeze that cooled sunburned cheeks, rumors of the Ole Goatman always crept into the tales.

"Have you ever seen him?" "Naw, no one has ever seen him." "He never leaves the thicket." "He ran away from his family." "He lives all by himself in that old shack with the goats." "His beard goes clear down to his chest."

We younger kids would draw closer together with eyes wide and ears straining. Nothing **TOO** scary was ever said, but a lot was left to the imagination. Sometimes I would get a little nervous and wished Mama would call me home for bedtime a little early. But I didn't dare leave till then 'cause I didn't want anyone calling me a *scardy* cat.

Fall Sunday afternoons meant it was time to head for the thicket to pick up pecans and gather red haws. The group always started out with lots of jokes and laughter, but as we came closer to the thicket, voices quieted and eyes were looking in all directions. The pecan trees grew at the edge of the thicket where the Goatman lived—or so the stories claimed. Maybe today would be the lucky day. Someone would actually catch sight of this mysterious man.

But it never happened, and when our sacks and buckets were filled, we'd head back across the gully, back to safety again.

One hot day in June I'll never, ever forget. I sat on the front porch, wondering what adventure might be waiting for me, when a thought struck right out of the blue.

"I think I'll just go check out that Ole Goatman. Just maybe I'll see if he's real or not." (Pretty big thinking for a seven-year-old.)

I headed across the field (of course, I didn't mention this to Mama) and went straight toward the thicket. After I scooted across the big pipe to the other side of the gully, I slowed down considerably, but I did keep going.

When I reached the pecans trees, I paused before edging into the deeper woods. The brush scraped at my bare legs. I couldn't hear any birds, in fact, I couldn't hear any sounds. It was too quiet. I thought, "Maybe I'd better go home now. Mama's probably worried."

Before I could get those pesky legs turned around, I heard a tiny, tinkling sound—a bell.

"Could it be a baby goat's bell? Maybe he's lost and needs my help."

I pushed aside a tall bush and peeked around. There, leaning against a tree, his face framed by scraggly hair and a beard not quite to his chest, stood the Ole Goatman. He looked at me with eyes that never wavered. It HAD to be him. Who else would be here and look like that?

A baby goat nuzzled his hand, but as if he were a specter of the woods, he never moved 'til a tiny twitch touched the corner of his mouth. That was enough for me! I turned and ran as fast as my legs would go. By the time I reached the gully, I was gasping for breath. I dared a quick look—nothing comin' back there—then scooted across the pipes to the other side, ran all the way home and collapsed on the porch steps.

I never told a soul. Sometimes I wondered if I really had seen him, or was it only a ghostly spirit of the thicket taking hold of my imagination.

After all these years, the mystery remains. "Who was he? Where did he come from?"

Over and over I've asked others, "Remember the Ole Goatman?" and if the person was a lease kid, the answer always comes, "Remember him? Do I ever!"

Last summer Emmett said he thought he <u>knew</u> him. In the '50s he came into town driving an old pickup truck to get food for the goats. But then, Emmett rethought this idea. That was another "goatman," who lived in the other direction.

I felt a kind of relief. Somehow the thought of "my" Ole Goatman driving a pickup truck put a crack in the mystique for me. I prefer to remember him as that man of mystery I "saw" in the thicket on a certain hot summer day.

Now, as I look back after 75 years of living, I ponder a greater mystery. What unthinkable tragedy would cause a person to choose the company of the goats over the closeness of family and friends? It's a riddle that I wonder about even today.

The Duck Lady

An Interactive Children's Story

How do you feel about Monday mornings?

Sometimes people seem to be a little slow on Monday mornings maybe because they're not quite ready to go back to work, or you kids may not be quite ready to go back to school. It's not because you don't like school. There might be something left over from the weekend you wanted to do. It just seems like sometimes we're not quite ready for Monday mornings.

Since we retired Mr. James and I kinda' look forward to Monday mornings, because we like to go to down to Middlefield to the big flea market. There are so many things to see down there, some old and some new, but all neat stuff.

Or may be the REAL reason we go is because they have the very best breakfast things to eat, especially the apple fritters and cinnamon rolls. Probably some people wouldn't call this the healthiest of choices, but we say it's OK sometimes. The last time we were there, I had a special treat. The Duck Lady was there sitting at the table right next to us.

She's a special, different kind of lady, who wears bright clothes and big hats. Another thing that makes her really special is that she always brings some of her ducks. Monday she had three—a brown one, a white one and a black one with a plume on it's head. She said it was the only plumed duck she's ever hatched at her duck farm. I could tell she was very proud of that duck.

Two of the ducks were sitting in a shopping cart, watching the people walking by. They would see the ducks and say things like, "Well, would you look at that!" and "Are those real ducks?" or maybe "Why would anyone put ducks in a shopping cart?" Some reached out to pet them. The ducks stayed very quiet and sorta' looked at the people as if to say, "What's the matter, didn't you ever see a duck in a shopping cart before?"

Others might notice the duck lady holding the duck with the plume, then just shake their head and walk away. I've talked with the duck lady a few times. She loves her ducks so much, and tells me all about them. She says each one is different even though to me, except for color, they look very much the same. But they are ducks and as the Duck Lady says, "God made them all."

I think people are a little like ducks. What do you think? Can you think of a single person who looks exactly like another person? Maybe twins, but even they are different in some ways. How are we different? Our hair, our eyes, our color; we're tall and short and some are a little thin, others not so thin. But in many ways, I guess we're alike. You can surely tell a person is not a duck, but we know God made each one of us. More than that, God didn't just make us, He made each one of us special. Can you think of something special about yourself?

Some of you can sing and some can dance. Some swim and some play games. Some tell stories and some like to read. There's so many things, but the most important thing is that no matter how different we are, God loves us every one. You know, Jesus said, "Let the children come to me," and later He said, "I am the Bread of Life." That means that he cares for us and just as we need food to be healthy and grow, we need Jesus to be happy and healthy as we think about who we are and what we want to do and be.

The Duck Lady cares for each of her ducks because each one is special to her. Jesus cares for each one of us because each one of us is special to him. He often uses Mamas and Daddies to help with this care. Right?

Jesus, thank you for sharing all the wonders of your creation with us. We know we are all different, and sometimes because of that, we get a little cranky with each other, but we thank you for always caring for us every day. Amen

From Rags to Rugs

A long time ago when things outside would get a little slow during my Illinois summer visit, I'd slip down the stairs to see what was happening in the basement. It was kind of an awesome (a word I certainly didn't use then) place. One corner was the absolute best because there was Aunt Lizzie's rag bin filled with a few whole pieces, but mostly there were strips of cloth separated into major colors. It seemed to me it was like a jumbled-up rainbow.

If I were lucky it would be a *weaving* day and I could watch my Aunt Lizzie at work. She was a large lady and I loved to watch her settle herself at the loom, look at me over her glasses and say, "Now, little Mildred, pick a few strips. What would you have me weave?"

After my choices from the rag bin, her fingers began to move. I never understood how the loom worked, but before long the rug began to take shape and color. Aunt Lizzie would interrupt the old gospel song she was humming, turn to me and say, "Hurry, girl, more strips, more strips. This loom is moving today." And the rag rug patterns would grow and change with each sweep of her arm.

Sometimes the rugs were summer bright and sang with the joy of reds and yellows. Others whispered of spring in quiet shades of blues and greens. Or they might be winter dark as shades of black mixed with strips of white snow.

I would skip from bin to bin choosing what caught my fancy. Bit by bit, with the magic of the loom and Aunt Lizzie's fingers, the rug would take shape and form; sometimes pretty, sometimes not, but always a surprise and different from the others.

Sometimes I would think I had chosen good colors, but only dullness came out. And I cried, "OH, Aunt Lizzie, I don't like it. Throw it away!"

"No, child, we'll keep it. It's done now and I'm sure we'll find a place for it."

Later I would find it under the dog, or outside the back door nearly covered with mud, or somewhere else, but serving a purpose.

Truthfully, I never made a rug, I was only the 'rag runner'; but somehow I felt a little ownership with each one. I had made a little difference with my choices.

Now as I think about it, I wonder if we aren't all weavers of sorts as our days come out of the loom of life. We choose the strips and feed them in. Like Aunt Lizzie's rugs, the tapestry is beautiful or drab depending on our strip choices, but there is always a place for them. I know there will be days of singing and I know there will be days of misery. But let me always remember the Master Weaver, who waits, no, who yearns to help me with the design.

Didn't He say in John 10:10, "I have come in order that you might have life--life in all its fullness." As I choose my daily strips, I live with this promise ever in my heart.

Mary Remembers — An Evening

Shalom—Please join me here in the stable. I'm Mary. I'm so glad you're here. Did you come because this is a night of remembrance? That's the reason I've come. As I sit here to have a few quiet moments, I've been remembering another very special night from what seems so long ago. But, other times it seems to me these strange and wonderful things happened only yesterday. May I share a few of my memories with you?

It all started when I was just a young girl in Nazareth. It was a very exciting time for me. I was betrothed to a fine carpenter whose name was Joseph. Then one night while I was dreaming about the future, suddenly an angel appeared. An angel! Now this was a very scary thing for me.

"My name is Gabriel," said the angel, "I have brought you a message from God. Don't be afraid, Mary." Well, how could I not be afraid. One doesn't have a visit from an angel every day. Especially one who claims to have a message from God; but he went on to say, "The Lord is with you and has greatly blessed you. You will have a holy baby, and He will be the Son of God. He will become a King and his kingdom will last forever."

I could only stare at the angel. How can this be? He said some more things and finally, because I didn't know what else to do, I said, "I am the Lord's servant, may it happen to me as you have said." The angel went away, and I sat there all by myself. My thoughts were very troubled and confused..

I was so puzzled. "The Mother of God's Son. Could there be some mistake? And what in the world would I ever tell Joseph?"

As it turned out, I didn't have to tell Joseph anything. An angel had come to him, too. He told Joseph about the baby and that his name should be Jesus. Everybody knew that a Messiah had been promised to our people of Israel for many, many years, but we still wondered about all of this. Could this really be happening to us?

I decided to visit my relative, Elizabeth, and found that she too was waiting for a baby. She said, "Mary, you have been chosen to have our Messiah. Truly you are blest." Later, I returned home to wait and wonder. It was reassuring that Joseph promised to be with me through all of this mystery.

There were Roman soldiers all over our country. Then Caesar, the Roman emperor, made a rule that everyone should register for a census count. Each person had to go to his own hometown to do this. This meant that Joseph and I would have to go to Bethlehem, which was 90 miles from Nazareth.

This was a problem, a big problem. You see, it was almost time for the baby to be born, and the long journey would mean riding on a donkey for almost a week. Phew—I tell you, I was really worried now. How could I do this, but God had promised to be with us.

We had no choice, so we put our faith in God's promise and headed south toward Bethlehem. The roads were crowded, and when we finally got to Bethlehem, I was very, very tired. Joseph looked everywhere for a place to stay, but there was nothing. It was growing later. I knew time was short.

"Joseph, we must find a place, any place," I begged him. "I think the baby will come tonight." Poor Joseph. What could he do? But again, God was with us. A very kind innkeeper offered what he had, "I have no rooms, but the stable out back is clean and will be warm. You can stay there for the night."

We thanked him and no sooner had we settled in than I knew the time had come. My baby would be born that very night. After the birth, we wrapped him in the special clothes we brought with us, and I sat near the manger as the baby, my baby, lay sleeping. We would call him Jesus just as the angel had told us.

The surprises for the evening were not over. Before long some shepherds came to the door of the stable. They hesitated as they looked inside.

"We are looking for the baby," they said. "Angels appeared over the fields, first there was only one who told us that the Savior, Christ the Lord, had been born in Bethlehem and was lying in a manger."

We were terribly afraid, but the angel said, "Don't be afraid." Then the whole sky filled with angels who were telling of the Good News and Peace on Earth. What a sight it was."

After they left, we knew we must see this thing that had happened. So we hurried straight here." I remember how the shepherds knelt down by the manger and said, "Truly, this must be the Son of God."

Well as you can guess, I was quite overcome. After the shepherds left, I held the baby close to my heart and wondered about all the things that had happened that very unusual night.

Did I know? Even though the angel had told me, did I really know that my baby was the Son of God. As Jesus grew, I knew He was a special boy; but how could I really know all that would happen. I must tell you this, that blest as I am, it has never been easy to be the Mother of the Son of God.

So as I sit here with you tonight, this I do know—Jesus brought a kind of love to the world that is unending. . .

. . . As Mary fades from my view, I focus on 'her' words--<u>a kind of love that is unending.</u> I can only try to imagine what her thoughts and feelings were on that night, but this I can be sure of--the kind of unending love that Jesus brings to the world is ours for the taking--only believe.

Mary Remembers — A Morning

The emptiness of my son's tomb was a reproach as well as a joy. After all, I should have realized more than anyone that he was no ordinary man. I should have seen that the days were leading to a resounding climax.

A man in brilliant garments appeared to us in the tomb and asked, "Why do you seek the living among the dead?" In that moment, I remembered another shining visitor, when I was just a maiden. He had tried to tell about the future. Now, I realized how much I misunderstood about my son.

What had that angel told me so many years ago? "He will be the Son of God, the Son of the Most High." I was puzzled, uncertain, how this could be, but my spirit rejoiced anyway. And the wonders of his birth! Shepherds arrived and claimed that angels had told them to come. Three strangers from faraway lands brought expensive gifts. They swore they were led to us by a star.

When we took him to be consecrated, an old man and woman exclaimed that God had allowed them to see the Messiah! *The Messiah!* Think of it. How long had the people waited for the Messiah?

Of course, Joseph and I marveled at these events, but eventually life resumed its ordinary course till suddenly, our lives were thrown into confusion again and it was with great difficulty that we made the arrangements to run away to Egypt. The angel again came with the message that we must leave with great haste if the life of our child were to be saved from Herod. It was two years before we dared to return to our homeland.

You may well ask if I discounted the unusual maturity and learning that my son displayed at the temple just twelve years after his birth. As first, I must admit, I was more concerned about the anxiety and inconvenience he caused us. After all, I was his mother.

Then I realized that well-educated rabbis not only asked my son questions, but eagerly awaited his answers! I pondered this as we trudged back to Nazareth; also, the way He reminded me that He was the Father's Son.

Once we returned to Nazareth, there were times as the years flew by that daily living seemed to crowd out the mystery of this son, Jesus.

Today, as I viewed these discarded grave clothes here in this tomb, I was deeply ashamed by the memory of that time I stood with his brothers in Capernaum. James and I, especially, despaired for his sanity over the things he was saying. We wanted to save our family from the humiliation of his madness. We tried to bring him home and keep him quiet.

His response to our pleas wounded me. He denied me, right there in front of the crowd. "Who is my mother?" He asked. "Whoever does the will of my heavenly father is my brother, my sister, my mother." I did not realize, even then, that he was not of this world.

Later as I wept at his cross, he did acknowledge his love and concern for me. He asked John to treat me as his own mother. He asked me to consider John as my son. In the midst of his excruciating anguish and humiliation, He held concern for me.

I wonder, "Did he know that I might more fully understand—here—in his empty tomb?"

Mary turns to leave the place of death, to seek her son among the living.

We, too, must seek the Son among the living if we are to know the promise of salvation.

PART FOUR

—

Other Stuff

Just A Little Mountain Church

The Great Smoky Mountains National Park and the surrounding area has been one of our favorite vacation choices for years. Gatlinburg was a quaint little town with a couple of country music shows on Saturday night. My uncle loved to go down from Illinois, find a rocking chair on Main Street and visit with anyone who would listen; and, there were plenty who would. Pigeon Forge was even smaller, with a couple of outlets and Craftsman's Alley.

As the years passed, more and more vacationers found their way to "my" place. Both of the towns changed, but the Park never changes. This does not mean that the towns were to be avoided but there was always the 'Park' with its incomparable beauty, trails to follow, the bears and other places to visit; it remains a tribute to the Creator. As the area grew, we didn't go as often, but remembered the location fondly. However, the last time I drove in downtown Gatlinburg, I was completely lost, trying to get to Pigeon Forge. How dare they "change things" on me?

Then one day, by accident, we found Cosby, a small town just east of Gatlinburg. The name rang a bell--more like sounded a gong. "Isn't this the place where your dad (Rev. John Dennis) was born?" James wasn't sure, but the next time we were in Oklahoma, we checked it out.

Sure enough. Not only was Dad born there, but it was his home 'til he was eight years old. James' great-great-grandfather, Thomas Caton, had been an itinerate preacher (sometimes called an exhorter) in the mountain area and was responsible, along with his son Stephen, for building a little church on a mountainside near Cosby. Dad had a very small picture of the church taken in 1952 when he had visited and preached there for a church family reunion.

That was all we needed and we decided we had to go back to Tennessee and find the church. We thought the name was Caton's Chapel. We tried the local store and several places and each one seemed to get us a little closer. Finally we found a school on Caton Chapel Road and figured "It's got to be around here someplace."

There was a little store near the school and this proved to be a lucky choice. One of the guys was very helpful. "Sure, I know where it is. Just turn left at the corner by the school and you'll come to the cemetery, and the church is about a quarter of a mile west of there."

He went on to tell us that his cousin, Dolly Parton, (yes, THE Dolly Parton) used to play there all the time. Her sister still lived just up the hill. He told another Dolly story: When she rode the school bus, she would make everyone sit down and be quiet because she was going to sing a song. Then she would sing all the way to school which happened to be several miles away. He did mention that not everyone was overjoyed with Dolly's singing.

Since I am a Dolly fan, I really enjoyed the stories. But we had to get on, so we followed his directions and sure enough, we found the church. Someone from the big house on the hill told us it was OK if we had a little picnic at the table by the church. I felt very comforted that we had found this place that had so much history of James' family woven into its story. I had been a little surprised that there weren't more "Caton's" resting in the cemetery but when we left, I waved a goodbye to the spirits that might be there.

The next spring, we were in Oklahoma and I was so excited telling Dad about finding the church in Cosby. As we talked, I was beginning to feel a little uneasy. I asked Dad if he still had a picture of the church.

Of course he did and the minute he gave it to me I saw something was wrong. "Dad, this isn't the church we found." The problem was no secret: there two churches--Caton's Chapel that was several miles north of Cosby; and the other one, Caton's Grove, that was a few miles west.

We had found Caton's Chapel, where Dolly Parton had played, but it had nothing to do with James' family. We needed to find Caton's Grove, the church that Thomas and Stephen Caton had built over a hundred years earlier.

It looked for sure that we just had to take another trip to Tennessee, and we did. This time we started asking questions west of town. We were sent to Serenity Falls, a beautiful waterfalls that sits right against the mountain and flows into Caney Creek.

This land had once belonged to Ed Caton (grandson of Thomas). In the early days, Highway 32 ran between Ed's house and Caney Creek at the bottom of the falls. There was a general store and grist mill and a few other buildings with the family home across the busy highway. To this day, traces of Highway 32 can be seen climbing the mountainside leading away from the "store."

The store was a central gathering place for the surrounding community and sold food and all the notions of a "general" store of the times until Highway 32 was relocated and many of the people moved. Ed Caton closed the store and he moved to West Virginia to work in the coal mines. Later he returned to the property and after his death, it remained empty for several years.

Eventually, Pattie and Ray Blackman (from Mississippi) bought the

property and began the mammoth job of turning the barn, the grist mill, the general store and Tillie's Stall into unique rental cabins. James and I stayed in the "general store" and it was an incredible experience. As we listened to the sound of Serenity Falls and Caney Creek flowing past the window, I felt as if we had been transported back in time to a far-away land. Pattie and Ray had done wonders with the restorations.

On Sunday morning, we visited the Caton's Grove Church service, and found a vital, faith-filled congregation.

There on the back wall was a picture of Rev. Thomas Caton, looking rather severe. But think of it, a clapboard building built in 1903, 110 years old, and still telling the story of Jesus. (I would think great grandfather Thomas should be smiling.)

A walk through the cemetery assured us that plenty of Catons and Dennises had lived in the area. One discovery was the correct spelling of James' middle name--Stokely. He always thought it was Stokley. He was named for his great uncle, John Stokely Dennis, who had married Dad's aunt, and was buried there. (I know, it gets confusing.) We decided the whole cemetery was just one big family.

We have returned to the church a few times for a visit and services. One Saturday night I asked James' newly discovered cousin, Paralee, "Who's talking at the service tomorrow?" Imagine my surprise when she replied, "Well, we hoped you would. You can, can't you."

"Um--well, O.K. I guess so."

And I did. I chose for my topic, "Surrounded by such a great cloud of witnesses . . ." Hebrews 12-1. During the service I felt such a deep closeness to this place where great grandfather Thomas, grandfather Stephen and Dad had all given words of guidance to God's children. Now for a morning, I dared to share the Good News of Jesus Christ. These were humbling moments for me, especially when the people were so gracious afterwards.

As you travel through the mountains of the southeast (and I'm sure elsewhere), you will catch glimpses of hundreds of these little white churches tucked away. Sadly, they are gradually disappearing, but when you do see one, please offer a prayer of thanks. For on such as these, a foundation of a country is built.

Let The Tears Fall

In great agitation my friend was brushing the tears from her cheeks. It didn't seem to help very much. They kept spilling over.

"This is so silly," she said.

Dear friend, don't apologize for your tears. I know there was a reason and it wasn't silly; therefore, neither were your tears.

When we stop to think about it, we may get misty-eyed for many reasons--not always the one that seems most obvious. When I crack my toe three mornings in a row on the bedpost, it's more the frustration at my continued 'klutziness' than the pain that brings the tears.

When I start sniffling frantically throughout the <u>Star Spangled Banner</u> at basketball games, it's not <u>all</u> because of our national anthem. Rather, it's the ghost from games past and a couple of players that keep dribbling across my blurred vision.

There are sizzling teardrops that sometimes seem the only solution to cool the waves of burning anger sweeping across the mind.

There are cool, sweet teardrops that come from happiness springs deep inside the soul.

There are tears that choke and tears that cleanse.

Children cry. We say, "don't" because you're too big. . . too old. . . it doesn't hurt. . . you're embarrassing me. . . "don't" and so we try to dam up the healing stream. The crying doesn't stop, it only flows inward.

Perhaps these are the most difficult, the tears that slash inwardly, like a cold winter rain, until they crest in a river of grief.

Jesus wept. So weep a little, my friend and let me share your tears. Through the sharing, we can reach that full blessing of laughter again.

So Afraid

"... and I am so afraid!"

Recently I read that fear is causing a greater number of problems among people than any other single cause today. We've become a world--not just a community, or even a nation--but a world of frightened people. Would an old fashioned way of saying this have more impact? We're *scared!* Even saying it is scary.

So, what do we fear? Nearly everything. When do we fear? Nearly all the time. Where? Nearly everywhere, even in our own front yard.

Strange that on the very day I read that first statement, I read something else. "Peace I leave with you; my own peace, I give you, do not be worried and upset, <u>do not be afraid</u>. I will care for you; I **do** care for you."

If you are thinking, "Those are the Lord's words," you're right. Maybe you're thinking something else--that they don't count for today.

This time, you're wrong. If they don't count, then what does? What can help us through the deep nights of our lives. If they don't count, then what can help us find a little joy in the morning, or a bit of rest in the hot afternoon? Are you satisfied with what does count for you today?

Surely you're familiar with the time Jesus walked on the water. (Matt. 14:22-32) But do you remember when impulsive Peter called out, "Let me walk, too," and when Jesus said, "Come," Peter tried it. He stepped right out and as long as he kept his eyes on the Lord, he moved with safe sureness. Later, he became afraid, took his eyes off Jesus, and began sinking.

You're thinking, just another *not for today* story. Wrong again.

There is an elusive element called faith available for living--it centers

89

on the Spiritual Being, and it grows within us until it permeates our whole lives.

With it, it's possible to walk on water. I've tried it, I took a few steps, I sunk, but with faith, I was willing to swim up and try again.

Why are we a people sinking in fear when we could be walking across the tops of these troubled waves waving a banner of faith? Is it really that simple? Yes, I believe it is that simple and that it speaks for today. Have you tried it?

Do I still have fear on occasion? Of course. But I know where to go for help when I remember these words, "Yea though I walk through the valley of death, I will fear no evil, for thou art with me." Ps 23:4

What Difference Does It Make?

I believe in Jesus Christ! "So," you think or maybe even say right out loud, "What difference does it make?"

"What difference does it make?"

Bobby Wilson was a real pain—to his mother, the neighbors, his friends, his teachers and anyone else who happened to cross his path. By the time he reached my data processing class, some were beginning to say, "Bobby is a hopeless case. He's headed for no good." Sometimes I wondered if they might be right.

There was no doubt about his abilities. When he wanted to, he could figure out computer problems that left me shaking my head. We had long uncomfortable talks in my office. Actually I talked, Bobby just sprawled in a chair and once in a while grunted, "So what?" or "What difference does it make?"

As time passed, his school suspensions and petty run-ins with the local police increased. A DUI charge brought probation, but somehow, he did manage to graduate. After graduation, I lost track of Bobby, but I did think of him occasionally and wondered what path he was on.

It was a few years later that I took a letter from my mailbox. The strange looking stamp on the corner of the envelope caught my attention. "Hm—Africa? Who in the world?" I tore it open and the signature scrawled at the bottom jumped out at me --"Bobby Wilson!"

I quickly scanned the message—"my wife and I are beginning our second year as missionaries in this African village," he wrote. "I'll bet you are surprised." (Stunned was more like it.) "I've been meaning to write you for awhile. I was in a lot of trouble after graduation, but I met this girl and through her, I found Jesus Christ (or maybe He found me). All I know is it has made a difference in every part of my life. I remembered all those talks in your office and I wanted you to know. I want you to know something else—those long talks made a difference, too. Remember, Jesus loves you."

As I wiped away the tears, I could only think, "WHAT a difference and I never knew."

What difference <u>does</u> it make to have the Lord present in a life? Let's look at what happened to some Old Testament people. There was Jonah who found himself in a whale's belly; Shadrach, Meshack and Abednego stood in a blazing furnace heated seven times hotter than usual; Daniel sealed in a pit with fierce lions; Queen Esther faced death because she was a Jew; and there's poor old Noah who was told to build a boat for the coming flood—but not only had he never seen a drop of rain, he didn't even know what it was.

Doesn't sound like a philosophy I would want to embrace. But these people put their trust in God and the whale spit Jonah out right on the beach; Shadrack, Meshack, and Abednego didn't even get singed; the lions became purring kittens; not only did Queen Esther escape death, but she saved her people and Noah, from the safety of the ark, watched it rain and rain. All of them put their trust in God and He made the difference.

Think of the story of Jesus as he began choosing his first disciples. Immediately Andrew ran to find his brother Peter, shouting, "I have found the Messiah!" What an announcement. In that moment lives were changed forever. (I wonder how long it has been since I have shouted, "I have found the Messiah?") These men began a journey that would take them up and down the dusty roads till finally they reached Jerusalem, and beyond to spread the good news of Jesus Christ, even to us right here today.

And of course, these chosen ones moved forward, never faltering in their faith, as they became perfect in their actions. Right? You know that is wrong. They had moments, even hours of doubt and despair, they argued and became jealous and angry with one another, their faith wavered dangerously. Thomas doubted the Master, Peter denied Him and Judas betrayed Him--Jesus forgave them all and <u>that</u> made the difference. Jesus understands our humanness and He forgives.

For most of us, to forgive a real or imagined wrong is almost always hard to do. Somehow we seem to want to hold the hurt close to us, to cling to that resentment of our ill treatment and finally the feeling turns into bitterness that can destroy us. These kinds of stress-based feelings push their way between family and friends, neighbors and co-workers and even split churches into hurting fragments.

And you know what, often all of this energy is so wasted because as you struggle with your mountain of pain, the other person may not even know how you feel or why. What a needless frustration. Instead, give it up, turn it over to Jesus, forgive as he forgives and let a brightness and joy return to your life. What a difference!

Does it seem to you that the anger held deep within the people of our world has never been so fierce? Day after day after day the news is filled with the tragic results of people lashing out in anger. From the playground to the neighborhood to the country to the world it goes on. It's an emotion we all feel sometimes—even Jesus became angry in the temple, but He can make a difference in the way we handle the anger. The killings and abuse are the headlines of destructive anger, but with the help of Jesus, we can redirect all this raw emotion and instead of blindly lashing out, it can become constructive anger and be used toward good. But it takes a brand new way of thinking—a "Jesus" way.

Perhaps one of the greatest differences that we experience in our belief is through receiving the love of Jesus. It a love which goes deeper that we can fathom, higher than any space shot could every reach, broader than any ocean we would ever cross and it stretches out into eternity and even then, it's only just begun. To know this love, one has to live it. Jesus shows us the way.

His love flowed ever outward—to the woman at the well, to the tired and hungry crowds on the hillsides, to the blind man, the leper, the cripple, the adulteress, the widow's son, to the woman on the street, the tax collector, the people of Jerusalem, the disciples and to us. There's no end to the stories telling of his love.

Faced with his own approaching death, Jesus' love spilled over again as He asked his father "…bless those who believe in me." He closed the prayer in John 17:26 by saying, "I made you known to them and I will continue to do so in order that the love you have for me may be in them, so that I also may be in them."

Have you walked with this love? Does it show through your daily life? We have an ever-present example of his love that we too often fail to take advantage of. We are surrounded by a world filled with color and sound that no artist can ever quite capture. The love lessons that can be learned through God's creation are without number.

Recently, Animal Kingdom presented a study of a mother cougar with her kittens. She cared for them with such tenderness, shielded them from harm, and patiently taught them survival lessons of the wilderness. I watched this outpouring of love and thought, "Dear Lord, you make the way of love so beautiful and so simple—if only every child could know such love, surely what a difference it would make to our weary world."

Thomas a Kempis said, "There is no creature, regardless of its apparent insignificance that fails to show us something of God's goodness." Would that we could open our eyes to these precious gifts from the Creator. Let them teach us the way of love.

Earlier I told you, "I believe in Jesus Christ" and it would have been fair for you to ask, "So what, does it make a difference?" It's a question I've asked myself. Maybe it's OK to ask.

After all, has this belief always kept me happy or safe from hurt or harm or shielded my children from the hateful ways of the world? Did it keep James' stroke from happening? As a very small child, did it stop the trauma of seeing my house in ashes, or watching that truck run over my beautiful dog who was my best friend? Did it keep my dad from dying with only half his allotted time lived? Did believing give me the wisdom to save the student who called me, then, with no hint, she hung up and took her own life?

The answer is NO to all of these questions. Believing did not prevent these tragic events from happening. I'm sure you have you own "why me" questions. These are the human experiences of life and we have NEVER been promised exclusion from them. They happen and they will continue to happen to all of us—believers and nonbelievers.

When I was about 10 years old, I sat in a persimmon tree, thought on things for awhile, and then decided it was time to accept Jesus as my savior and be baptized. In all of Oklahoma there was only one pastor who belonged to the church of my grandfather. Even though he didn't live nearby, I wanted him to baptize me. So, we went to him and I was baptized in a swimming pool in his town.

As I climbed up the ladder and out of the water, I felt happy and I thought, "Now I'm really good! I'm sure I'll never sin again." Before we were out of town, I discovered that's not the way it works.

So what difference <u>does</u> all this make? One thing I know for sure— through Jesus Christ as a source of power in my life, I have found a comforter, a counselor, a teacher, a friend, and a savior who accepts me and loves me just as I am. And this is the difference, because I know him, I will try to live as he would have me live. Sometimes it works, sometimes not, but in the presence of his power, it is possible to keep on trying.

I know with great certainty that in my deepest sadness, joy will return; in despair, hope will shine; and in every way, when I am most fragile, He strengthens me and makes my life very much worth the living. Jesus once said, "I am come that you might have life, and that you might have it more abundantly." What a beautiful promise—to have life more abundantly. But it's a challenge too.

Dare to look deep within your innermost self. Are you letting Jesus make an abundant difference in your life? Or is something clogging the path of that abundance?

Is it foolish pride, or an unforgiving attitude, a resentment or bitterness or maybe destructive anger? Perhaps you are thinking, "But life is good for me right now. I like me just the way I am. I won't bother the Lord." But can you truly say, "Life couldn't be better." Think again. You don't have to settle for <u>better</u>; his promise is <u>abundant</u>. The promise is His, the challenge is yours.

Like Andrew, I would rush to you today and exclaim, "I have found the Messiah!" He is a risen Lord who stands beside you, ready to walk with you. Don't turn away. Invite Him to come along on this life's journey.

What difference does it make? Only you can give the answer for you. Jesus will give you the 'stuff' to make it happen.

And Away We Go

Is there anyone out there who hasn't taken some kind of road trip? Even a small one? Well, that experience seems to be rather high on our list of things to do, and sometimes lands us in some very unusual circumstances.

It all started after the wedding, the evening of the honeymoon. It was raining and already dark when we left the reception. Of course, I asked James where we were headed. "You'll see," he laughed. About two hours later, I kind of figured it out, as we approached his old hometown, Kingston, OK. There was a lodge on Lake Texoma, The Willows, and we drove back to it. All was dark and the sign said, "Closed for the season." (February).

By now it's getting toward midnight and our *honeymoon* was approaching day two. He said, "Don't worry, I know another place." and he did. It was a small motel, The Honeymoon Lodge—one room and a bed, but then what more did we need? After all it WAS a honeymoon.

We left early the next morning, and had two more days before I had to go back to school. Got almost home and ,"Whoops, what's that funny noise?" As it turned out, the car wheels were out of alignment and the front right tire was worn to shreds. Luckily we were less than a mile from my Mom and Dad's house. The unlucky part is James used his flight money to buy the new tire we needed. Nothing to do but borrow the money needed to fly to Seattle for shipping out for Korea. I did get the loan repaid before he got home again.

I'm sure all of you readers have experienced trip adventures with your kids. Johnny was our "trip adventure" boy. The scariest time happened when he was about three. Somehow he climbed the stone barrier at Kentucky Dam and while looking over to see the bottom of the dam, he started slipping. Our friend caught his heel just as he started over.

Now I know you're thinking, that we never watched him close enough, but that kid was quicker than greased lightning. About the same age (maybe the same trip) we missed him in middle Missouri while making a refueling stop. The kids got out for all the usual gas station reasons, but when we were ready to leave, Johnny was missing. After some frantic searching, I heard a motor down the street. Following the sound, I found him, walking up and down behind a man with a lawn mower.

Exciting happenings can only describe our trip to New England. It began with a roadside amusement rest stop when John's leg caught in the rails on the outer caboose platform of a train. Of course his howling thoroughly embarrassed his brother and sister when I tried to pull the leg free. Just when I was ready to go look for someone to 'saw' him out, he gave a little twist and said, "Look at that," then galloped off in another direction.

We missed him on the Atlantic coast; James finally found him in the back of a cave just as the tide was coming in filling the cave with ocean water. He could never have gotten out by himself. He told his dad he had to "check out those anemones."

A word of caution about bridges--never believe the "Bridge of Flowers" signs that line the Vermont highways. I persuaded James to go 50 miles down and 50 miles back to enjoy the advertised beauty. Nothing--the bridge was not much longer than the one over the Grand River and there was not one flower--wrong season? At each end was a tiny, sickly evergreen bush--that was it.

It was quiet in the car as we drove back to our highway, but the kids have never let me forget this memorable experience.

Another bridge to avoid is the famous "Free Bridge" into Mexico, again advertised for miles along the Texas Rio Grande. Since we'd never been into Mexico, I thought this would be good learning experience. It was!

We crossed the bridge, drove across the flowing Rio Grande—actually about 10 feet wide at this point. After a couple of miles, saw nothing, then turned around to come back into the good old USA.

As we approached the bridge, a Mexican official in uniform stepped out of a little building in front of the car, and asked us for the toll. But this is the 'free bridge,' the signs said so. Here's the catch. <u>For those who wish to cross into Mexico, it's free; but for those who wish to return to the USA, it is NOT free.</u> James fumed a bit while I'm saying, "Pay him, pay him!!!" That was our one and only entry into Mexico.

A word of warning—maps are not always to be trusted. In southern Maine we found ourselves on a traffic circle that indicated more than one exit. Not so. After following the circle several times, a truck driver finally got us headed south again. California exit signs are impossible—the only way they point is straight down. For sure, I did not want to go straight down.

Another time we were coming out of Tombstone, AZ (a neat town) running a little late. I looked at the map and told James we could save several miles by taking this shortcut. So, we turned east and things were going well, until the road turned into gravel and we began crossing cattleguards. Definitely Not Good! When the road became dirt, I began to fidget and wondered if we'd missed something. Still, poor as it was, the road had to be going somewhere, so we kept driving at a speed painfully less than the one posted on the Interstate. Finally after miles and miles, I caught a glimpse of something in the distance besides tumbleweeds. Gradually the road turned back to gravel, then blacktop; we made a big curve and there before our eyes was a town—well, that may be stretching it a little—more like a village with a convenience store and filling station. A little further on at the end of "Main Street" was an I-10 entry ramp.

That same I-10 gave us a real problem in San Antonio—this time not my fault. We had completed and enjoyed the Spanish Mission Driving Tour and were ready to move on. The dirt side road was fenced off from the Interstate—no entries. Finally we came to a place where the fence was down with tracks crossing over. James drove across the bar ditch and we made our own entry—just in front of the Texas highway patrol. He was tearing down the highway, so he must have been on another call, because he ignored us completely. Or maybe the downed fence was a legitimate entry to I-10. One never knows in the Southwest.

James wasn't so lucky when he ran the Oklahoma highway patrolman off highway 70 late one night. We didn't know there had been highway work; lines weren't marked yet. James was passing another car, just as the patrolman topped the hill. All three cars were in a row—the other car, our car on the highway, and the patrolman off the road very near the ditch. We drove on, and it didn't take long for the flashing lights to appear behind. I'll never know why, but for some reason (I'm sure the only time in his life) James was driving barefooted, and when he had to step out of the car, there he stood with feet shining.

Obviously shaken, the patrolman's words were, "Man, do you know you ran me off the road?" I'm thinking "Well, dah!" but for once I kept my mouth shut. James settled the fine with a check for $25, which the patrolman put in a big envelope, said "Watch it" and returned to his car. We let him pull out ahead of us, before traveling on.

One more sign to watch for—"Road Closed Ahead." They are not always closed if you have a copilot with you who is willing to move the tree that fell down and ford the creek where the bridge seems to have washed away.

Those Smoky Mountain Roads can be treacherous, especially the one over the mountains from Cherokee to Gatlinburg in the spring. With a temperature of 45 degrees, we started up with no qualms, even though it was dark. As we climbed, the temperature dropped along with the unexpected snow. I kept driving slower and slower, and the snow fell faster and faster, along with the thermometer. I followed the lights of another snow bird until they turned. I didn't turn because my fingers were stuck in one position—from fear. I don't know where that lead car ended up, but fortunately we were on the road. Finally we started down, the snow slacked off and after a few more miles, it was a balmy 45 degrees again.

We grabbed some burgers and found a motel. The lady took one look at me and said, "I'd bet anything you just came over the mountain, didn't you." I could only shake my head. "Nobody does that at night this time of year," she laughed. I could only think, "No kidding? Well, we sure won't do it again."

When we were young and foolish, we never made motel reservations—James said we didn't know where we might be, and he was right; but this makes life interesting at times. It's not supposed to snow in southern Maine in April, but late this night it did—kind of a spring blizzard on a pretty much deserted highway.

Finally we saw a small light that flashed "Lodging." Actually the guy was closing up, but agreed to fix us some sandwiches and said he had a place we could stay. The "place" was around back under his garage. Again a room with a bed, a bathroom, and a postage-sized TV which got one station. We really didn't need the TV except maybe to get a weather report.

We ate our sandwiches and went to bed. Happily there were plenty of covers. Better than one night when we slept in the car and I got so cold I put on an old pair of James' coveralls to keep warm. To be fair, this was on a fishing trip, but I had been promised a motel..

Did you know there are motel cabins in the Black Hills that have no locks on the doors? We'd already paid and carried in the stuff, when we discovered that. A chair propped under the doorknob worked. At least no one carried us off in the night. I did have some red bites on my body the next morning. Bug bites? I don't know, but they are gone now.

Probably the most interesting place we've stayed was in Lebanon, Mo. We were on kind of an emergency trip and had been driving for some time. By now, it was quite late and I told James I needed to get some sleep if I were to be coherent the next day.

Finally we found a motel off Rt. 66 on the bypass to Lebanon. The name <u>Foxy Lady</u> should have told me something, but I went in and asked for a room. When he asked if I wanted it for just an hour, bells should have gone off. But I said, "NO, till morning." He looked at me kinda funny, but took my money and sent me to the room.

It was clean, with a bath and a bed—nothing else. No chair, no phone, no dresser, no desk. Finally it dawned on me—Oh no, could this be one of those 'bad places'? But we needed the sleep, so we said "OH WELL"

101

and went to bed. I woke up a couple of times when I heard cars coming and going during the night, and there was a different car next door when we left—but any port in a storm, right?

You've heard the expression, "small world"? Well, you have no idea. We were racing down a back road in east Texas when a sign pointing up a side road read, <u>Ladies Outlet</u>. I slammed on the brakes, backed up and made a right turn. Back in the field under the piney woods was a house with the Outlet sign again. "Look at that, James, a Lake County car." I ran inside, where several women were shopping and called out, "Who's here from Lake County?" A voice from a dressing room answered, "I am," and she came out partly dressed, looking for me. Turned out she was from Madison (the town right next to Perry), and though we didn't know each other, we had several friends in common.

Another time we stopped at the east-end rest stop of the road through the Badlands. You guessed it. Another Lake County car. Again, we didn't know them, but their son-in-law worked at the Perry Schools and we talked to him all the time when we went to swim. After we got home, he thought it was funny that we had talked with his mother-in-law in the South Dakota Badlands.

Probably the most unusual "small world" happening was being greeted by the Hawaiian girl with orchid leis when we landed in Hawaii. She asked where we were from. "Oh, yeah, Perry; close to Mentor, right?" We couldn't believe she had worked with our son-in-law at the 3-M Company. I know you've had your own *small world* memories.

I am a fairly reliable driver as long as I'm going straight ahead. Backing is another story. Several years ago, a young Donna and I went to pick strawberries at West's orchard. Leaving Donna in the patch, I took the berries to the car, and decided to park our new Oldsmobile a little closer. I backed right into a pole that "someone had moved behind me" and crumpled the fender. I was so distraught, I drove straight home, leaving Donna in the strawberry patch. I called James at work and through many tears, told him what happened. To his question, "Where's Donna," I first said "I don't know," then, "Oh gosh, she's still in the strawberry patch." When I went back to get her, she simply asked, "Where ya' been, Mom."

I sat on the curb and cried the whole time Bill Smith Olds was making the estimate.

Other dings—backing into the dumpster (new car) at a California restaurant, trying to knock down the drive thru at a Picayune Mississippi bank. (I just took my money and left quickly.) At least, I didn't back into Donna's brand new car with the truck in our own driveway as someone who shall remain nameless did or another time crumple the front end of a friend's new car like an accordion.

The newfangled bells and whistles don't always help—especially in the desert when the low-tire light comes on, but what really needs to be done is to let some air OUT, because the tires are overheated.

Over the years, as we've traveled in 49 of the 50 states one of the true joys has been seeing and visiting so many churches. There's a little blue church sitting by the wayside in Canada where we didn't stop. I've thought about that church and always regretted that we passed it by. There was a church in Appalachia with an altar rail so used that the varnish was completely worn away. Still, I found it was very possible to kneel and say a prayer.

One of the most inspiring Easters we've enjoyed happened at a small church on the New Jersey coast. During the Easter celebration, a member rose to give his testimony. He told of his cancer healing, thanking the people for their prayers and the Lord for sparing him. As he sang "He Arose" my own spirit soared with rejoicing. I learned after the service that this was his first Sunday back since his illness began.

We found the little Methodist church in Caton's Grove, Tennessee built by James' great grandfather, the Exhorter Thomas Caton. It sits right at the edge of the Great Smoky Mountains National Park and is still used for worship today. We were there one Saturday night, talking with a distant cousin. I asked, "Paralee, who's speaking at church tomorrow?" She replied, "Well, Millie, we hoped you would. You will, won't you?" And somehow, with the Lord's help I did. That was a such moment—to be in that place, beside the Caton cemetery where Thomas and so many other Catons and Dennises rested. To think that James' great grandfather, his grandfather, and his father had all shared the message of God's love there.

And then, "surrounded by so great a cloud of witnesses," I was blest to share the same message.

Recently we had a little reunion in Birmingham. James had two army buddies who had been a part of our wedding. One was the best man. That was 61 years ago and we hadn't seen them since that day. Nor had they seen each other. With the help of "people search" I found both of them. They lived near Birmingham where Rick lives, so we got together for lunch and lots of stories. You WOULD not believe. But this was such a joy of our travels.

James and I never begin a journey without inviting an extra passenger to ride with us. Surely God's guardian angel has watched over us in our travels, both good times and bad. Sometimes I think maybe we've put a little strain on the asking, but we know God is always with us.

We live in such a beautiful country and I wonder if sometimes we forget to treasure it.

To Be A Teacher — Just Imagine

The halls were tomb quiet and in the subdued lighting, the rows of open lockers gaped like ancient mummy cases. It was Day 370--two years had passed since that first day. The last bell of 1951-52 had sounded, the students were gone leaving behind a few scattered papers littering the hallway and left-over memories lingering in the air. For me, it was the end of a momentous two years of my life.

The August sun (1950) had dawned Oklahoma hot. No matter, I'd been awake for hours. College graduation was a dream ago behind me. The present was NOW. The 15 high school students sitting in front of me were the reality of the moment. With eyes never blinking, they sat and waited and waited.

I could only think, "OK, what do I do now with all the waiting teenagers?" I was only two years away from "teenager" myself, so why the shaking knees? I shuffled the lesson plans I'd carefully worked out, and finally, in what I hoped was a strong voice, I ventured, "Good morning, class. I am your new teacher, Miss Murphy."

The eyes, still not blinking implied a strong, "So?" And so it began, my first year of teaching.

Centerview was a small consolidated school in central Oklahoma. The brick high school building (courtesy of the C.C.C.), the clapboard grade school and gym, superintendent's house and a very small duplex (with one bath) which I shared with another teacher and three children sat on the sandy campus. A baseball field, some swings, a slide and merry-go-round completed the site. Two small country stores and gas stations served the needs of the extended community.

The student body was a hodge-podge of humanity--Sac and Fox American Indian, Polish American and children of locals who farmed the sandy land, raising mostly peanuts.

Because I had attended a small consolidated school in an oil patch town only 40 miles away, this part was not new to me. My own student body had also been a hodge-podge--oil lease kids the majority, completed by rancher and farm kids, a couple of Indian families and the 'town' kids.

As the first few weeks passed, it was usually very quiet in my room as I struggled to make typing, bookkeeping, shorthand and a couple of English classes the most interesting challenges these kids had every faced. (I know now that it was my very good fortune that I didn't have to compete against the distractions of television and cell phones.)

My superintendent, Mr. Spencer, had talked with me before the beginning of school. "Miss Murphy, you are a very young, small person. You are going to have to be <u>very firm</u> with these students. You must establish yourself as the boss."

He didn't give me a lot of hints on how to do this. I thought it meant, "Don't smile. Never joke with the students. Present the lesson in a strong, business-like way."

It didn't take long to discover this wasn't working very well. I was making little headway with getting to know the students, and I felt the learning level on a scale of one to ten was zero.

One night in my little one room duplex which included sleeping and cooking space, I began to think of my own high school days. I remembered how much I looked forward to going to school almost every day. I remembered the teachers and how they were. A light kind of came on.

The next day I started a whole new approach and I said to each class,

"Let's get to know each other." I shared a few things about myself, what I liked and didn't like. Then I said, "Now it's your turn."

Even though there had been a couple of smiles as I shared my stories, the eyes were still questioning. Finally, someone broke the ice by sharing that she liked barrel racing. I asked about her horse and the fun of competition; then someone else spoke up.

There was a different feeling in the air as we returned to "typing time." (I remember years later when one of my students said to me, "Mrs. Dennis, you're just like a real person." Probably one of the best teaching compliments I ever received.)

Because the school was small (less than 100 students) it wasn't many days before I knew something special about most of them. It was about a month later that Cowboy Rice, a senior Sac and Fox student, who was something of a leader for all classes, stayed after the bell rang and said, "Hey, Miss Murphy, could I tell you something?"

"Of course, Cowboy, what is it?"

"Well," he stumbled a little, "we think you're OK."

Before I could say anything, he left the room and my next class was coming in."

But those words set a new tone. Things became more relaxed in classes and I felt for the first time that learning was going on. Of course, it wasn't perfect, but so very much improved.

Just as I was beginning to relax, in October, Mr. Spencer came to me with a total surprise. "Miss Murphy, we are closing school for a couple of weeks, so you can have a little vacation."

"But why are we closing the school?"

"The students are needed to shake the peanut crop for the next two weeks. You are free to do whatever you want."

I'd never heard of shaking peanuts and I'm still not sure how that works, but I decided to go home for a change. Then came another surprise. Because of the little "police action" going on in Korea, my boyfriend was being drafted into the army. I waved goodbye to him at the bus station as he headed for Ft. Sill before being stationed for training at Camp Chaffee, Arkansas.

A week later, the peanuts were "shook" and I was back in the classroom. Another surprise! Mr. Spencer said, "Miss Murphy, since you have been chosen the Junior Class sponsor and you are the English teacher, we need you to direct this fall's Junior Class play."

"But, Mr. Spencer, even though I was in a couple of plays in *grade* school, I've surely never had any training in anything like that. I don't know . . ."

"Oh I'm sure you'll do a fine job. Maybe Mrs. Shadden (the other English teacher) can give you some pointers. I have some books you can look at and we'll order the play you'd like to do."

"Thanks, I think." I looked at the books and talked to the Juniors. Surprisingly, they were interested and some were excited about the whole idea. I finally chose a play I'd seen once, "Aaron Slick From Punkin Crick," and we began.

This meant in between teaching, lesson plans (due every Friday afternoon) and grading papers, I spent later afternoons and/or evenings with the students practicing the play. Finally the time came, and we gave performances on Friday and Saturday nights. With little else to do, we had good crowds and the kids received standing ovations. Of course there were several parents, grandparents and friends in the audience. I was very proud of them. When it was over I felt so good about the whole experience that I directed a reprieve in an Illinois school about ten years later.

I settled into a routine and there HE was again. "Miss Murphy, our small library is a mess. I'd like for you to take over, get the books in some kind of order, then oversee the operation so the students can use it more to their advantage."

By this time, I didn't even consider the option of a "No" answer. I just went to work. The "library" consisted of few shelves along the study hall wall with a few books. Except for the fact that I read a lot, I knew very little about library organization. I recruited four girls who also liked to read as helpers, found a book on the Dewey Decimal system and we began to catalog and shelve the books in our spare time. By the end of the school year, it had the semblance of a not great, but certainly useable library.

As we moved through the month of April, the kids began to talk about the Junior/Senior trip. I listened with interest, but didn't give it much thought until . . . yes, there He was again. "Miss Murphy, you know the Junior/Senior trip is coming up soon. This year the kids will be going to the Sulphur Park for a Friday and Saturday night, coming back on Sunday afternoon. Of course, as Junior Sponsor, you will be joining the Senior Sponsor for the trip."

This pretty much threw me for a loop. I had just turned 21 when I started teaching. Some of the students were 19. Although our relationships had come a long way in the classroom, I wasn't at all sure I felt qualified to be responsible for almost 30 high school students for a two-night trip. (My teacher-training classes didn't have a chapter on this topic. In fact, I was discovering there were several topics my teacher-training classes had neglected to mention.)

But, as always, there was no question, I would go. Actually as it turned out, the trip went well with only a few speed bumps and I had a pretty good time. We stayed in two dormitory-type cabins and did our own cooking, some on outside fires. I discovered a couple of the girls and one of the boys were much better cooks than I. In retrospect, considering my cooking abilities, that isn't saying too much.

Although everyone was a little frazzled with sleep the number one priority, we arrived at Centerview Sunday afternoon. The group of parents waiting for pickup seemed happy to greet their kids, and I know that little duplex looked good to me.

Before long, I was sitting in the gym watching the Seniors graduate. I had so many conflicting thoughts as I watched each one cross the stage. Each one left an imprint in my memory to be treasured--some good, some not so good--but all a part of that "first year."

I went home during the summer and had my first really quiet time since I had started to college. It was a summer apart as I discovered what "vacation" really means. People asked me, "How do you like teaching?" Usually I gave the standard "It's OK." Truthfully, I was still thinking about it, "Was it right for me and the students I would touch?"

I did make one big decision that summer. I decided to buy a car. With Daddy's help, I found a used car that seemed to fill the bill, and if

I could borrow $1,000, I could pay cash for it. My teacher's salary for the first <u>year</u> had been $2,000. I had saved some of that and was getting a raise for the second year--$2,400. I talked with Mr. Spencer and he agreed to loan the $1,000. I would pay him back with $100 each month of the school year. When I pulled into my little space beside the duplex in August, I turned off the engine and just sat there. My own car--it was almost too much to believe.

The first semester was so much easier than the year before. I knew almost all of the students and usually knew what to expect from them. I'd been through the classes and needed only to improve on what I taught the previous year.

I thought, "This isn't so hard. I think I really like it." Then about six weeks into the year, the absolutely unexpected, unthinkable thing happened. It was hard!

During the Senior Typing class, I would sometimes walk up and down the rows observing the student's typing form, answering individual questions and helping on a one-on-one basis. One afternoon, the oldest boy in the class stopped, and very quietly said "Miss Murphy."

"Yes, Bobby. You have a question?"

Even more quietly, without any hesitation, he suggested that I meet him that evening out behind the gym, and told me in no uncertain terms, what he had in mind for us.

I've always been a person who seldom became really angry, or lost my temper. But I became a person possessed. I drew back and without a thought, I knocked him right out of his chair. Then I turned and walked out of the room and straight to Mrs. Spencer's office. Fortunately, he was in.

I was so **mad** I could barely speak, but finally was able to tell him exactly what had happened. I went on to say, "I want that boy out of my room NOW!!!! Mr. Spencer was very understanding and asked me if I thought I could go back to my room.

"Yes, after he is out."

We walked down the hall together and he took Bobby out. (He was back in his seat) The students sat in total silence. Nothing was said until the bell rang and the students left. Fortunately it was the last class of the day.

After school ended and the kids left, Mr. Spencer and I talked about the incident. I was still very shaken about what had happened; it seemed my "teaching world" had kind of toppled.

But we agreed on a plan: Bobby stayed out of class one more day, then after he and I talked, he apologized. By then, I had regained my senses, apologized for hitting him, and we agreed the problem was ended.

I never struck another student in all my years of teaching. I wouldn't recommend it, even for that situation, especially in today's world. As I've thought about it, I wish it hadn't happened, but there's no way I could have handled it differently on that day at that time.

Year's later I ran into one of the girls who had been in the class. "You know," she laughed, "I'll always remember when you knocked Bobby right out of that chair. We've always wondered what he said. The thing is, someone should have done it a long time before then."

After Thanksgiving, my one chance at coaching basketball came up. Mr. Spencer had a new idea. "Miss Murphy, we lost our girls' basketball coach over Thanksgiving. I know you played basketball in high school and I'd like you to take over."

I had neither the good sense nor the courage to say no.

Oklahoma has always taken its basketball very seriously on all levels. The Centerview girls team had had a very tough year with NO wins. Using a few borrowed plays and some remembered from my own experience, we began. Actually, I didn't do any worse than my predecessor--my team didn't win either. They did play hard and lost one game by only one point.

One problem did develop. Remember the guy who was drafted? Well, he came home in January and said he was being sent to Korea in two weeks. He followed that bombshell with another: He asked me to marry him the next Sunday. Of course I said, "Yes." (I could hardly believe it, I'd been chasing him for almost five years.)

Here's the problem--my basketball team was playing in the county tournament on Friday night. If they won, they would play again on Saturday night. I was really in a "funk." I wanted them to win, but I didn't know what I would do if they did.

Friday night came. They played their best game of the year, but they didn't let me down. They lost, and my Sunday wedding went off on schedule. Mr. Spencer gave me three days off for a 'honeymoon' and the next week gave me Thursday and Friday before my new husband left for Korea on Saturday night.

Miss Murphy became Mrs. Dennis and both the students and I had some trouble keeping my "name" straight.

Someone asked me once if I got lonely living in that little duplex on the school campus. But, how could I? In addition to all the class preparations, I was, from the beginning, a teacher who believed if work was given to be handed it, then it deserved to be graded. All of my classes required a "ton of paper" work. Then just when things would quiet down, here came Mr. Spencer with a new job to be done.

The last one: Mrs. Dennis, I'm sure you would do an excellent job heading up the Junior-Senior Banquet this year. We'd like it to be special. The Junior students can help you."

It <u>was</u> and kind of a goodbye for me, too. As it turned out that was my last year at Centerview. I was moving to Illinois to live.

What did it mean to me? As the years passed and I went on to other schools in Illinois and Ohio, I often look back on those first two years. I was so lucky to have students who challenged me in so many ways and a superintendent who let me try things on my own, but was always willing to redirect me when I got lost.

My Grandmother came to my college graduation from Illinois. While she raised eight children of her own, she taught in one- and two-room schools for over 20 years. After the ceremony she put her arms around me and whispered, "Mildred, to be a teacher is such a special thing; but only if <u>you</u> make it so.

Grandma, in my 35 years of teaching, I've tried hard "to make it so."

With the constant presence of the Master Teacher as my guide, I believe it's been special for most of my students, and I know it's been special for me. I believe I owe a lot of this to my Centerview post-grad training; a tiny school in the  middle of nowhere that had such an overwhelming influence on my life and thus, on the lives of so many others. I do thank God for that.

Could it have happened anyplace else? I don't know. I only know this is the way it was for me in that place--that Oklahoma. JUST IMAGINE!

PART FIVE

—

Family Living

A Daughter Is One Who . . .

This is a message of hope to all long-suffering mothers of daughters. I know many of you are much more qualified than I, but I have been there.

I remember as if it were yesterday. That beautiful baby who laughed and cried, emptied her bottle and pooped her diaper and I thought, "When will she please grow up just a little? Soon, please."

Then it happened . . . she began to grow and there she was, a little girl who clung to my leg till people began to wonder if she was a permanent fixture.

One who screamed at the sight of a comb and convinced her father that she was being tortured every morning before leaving for kindergarten.

One who could spend an hour choosing which dress to wear to school, from the two we had spent an hour choosing the night before.

One who could change a mood from a soft summer breeze to a hard northerner in less time than it takes to turn around and all with no apparent reason.

One who could do walkovers and round-offs with the grace of a ballerina, but couldn't walk down our short hall without bouncing off the wall at least twice.

One who could eat ice cream, pizza, and macaroni and cheese every day, and was convinced that God gave us the green vegetables only for rabbits.

One who could pick up a whispered secret through three closed doors, but couldn't hear "Pick up your room" shouted across a small hall.

One who could always find one more perfectly reasonable (to her) way to ask, when the answer was already a definite "No!"

One who could giggle and cry at the same time without a reason for either.

One whose constant, boundless energy often left me gasping for breath and who, time after time. left me with a feeling of total bewilderment and wondering, "Now, how did she outmaneuver me again?"

One who just kept on growing and one day I found myself thinking, "When did this happen , Lord? She's not a little girl anymore?" And one more time she's outmaneuvered me.

So where is the message of 'hope'?

I can't believe she's a 'woman' now. Where did the years go is such a cliché, but where **did** they?

I've always treasured her as a daughter, but over the years another surprise has 'snuck up' on me. More and more, I value her as my friend-- fun to be with, nice to know.

Red Dirt Mama

When Mama stepped off that Greyhound bus into Daddy's waiting arms, she never could have imagined the drastic changes waiting for her. Depression remained very much a part of many lives in 1933 and it was the reason for the move from the flat, black farm land of central Illinois to the red dirt oil patch of Seminole, Oklahoma. Oil was the magic word as rivers of the sticky, black stuff was discovered under the 'worthless' land. Suddenly hundreds of men were needed to tame the gushers and refine the gas.

The groans of the '29 Ford as it climbed the red, rocky hill were nothing compared to Mama's groans when she saw the boomshack—unpainted shot-gun structures thrown together for the families of the workers who came.

From a two-story farm home to two tiny rooms, a closed-in back porch and a path was a stretch, but if nothing else, Mama was a survivor and after a few days, she jumped right in. Daddy's new job at the Sinclair gasoline plant provided a little money to buy paint and paper to "fix up" the bare walls. The new wall paper also helped keep out the blowing wind.

In amazement she watched real water running into the kitchen sink, the glow of a bulb with the pull of a string, and a cook stove that burned natural gas. All of the oil companies provided these *luxuries* for their employees at no cost. Learning new rules for cooking took awhile. For years, I thought three pots were part of the recipe necessary to cook the Saturday beans—one to burn them, a second to burn them again and the last one to finish them.

Mama was outgoing and quickly settled into lease-living. She often joined the gathering under the cottonwoods as the other Mamas shared stories of growing up all over the country. Her two main worries were that I would fall into the slush pits near the oil wells or that I might get too close to 'the Indians'. (Remember, she was a pilgrim in the 'wild, wild west'.) As time passed, she discovered that these 'different' people could be good friends, too.

She was homesick for her family and after a couple of years, when Daddy got his first vacation, we were off to Illinois for a visit with the relatives. She packed as much visiting into the two weeks as possible, then waved goodbye to Grandma and her brothers and sisters. Through her tears, she knew she was ready to go back to her 'adopted home.' On the way, she often mentioned how glad she was that someone had finally paved that dusty old road (the Mother Road, Route 66) since her bus trip down.

Two days later darkness had settled as we reached the top of our hill. What a fearful sight! One jagged, charred post stood like a sentinel in the moonlight. Fire! The scourge of the oil patch had swept down the row of houses and three (including ours) were burned to the ground. We stood ankle deep in the ashes and twisted metal. Mama's new Montgomery Ward stove and icebox, our clothes, our memories—everything was gone. Of course, Mama cried but even as Daddy wiped her tears, she was already planning how she could fix-up the next shotgun house. (I think it says something for their faith and optimism when just slightly over nine months later my baby sister, pesky June, arrived.)

After staying with friends, for a few weeks, another boomshack was vacated on the lease; we moved in and the fix-up began. With Mama, it was like that with all the houses (there were seven over the lease years, only two with indoor bath facilities).

A tornado blew away the roof from one; another had only two rooms and with a new baby sister, we were pretty crowded; an all-night hail storm shredded the roof on one and Mama's new paper fell off in strips. It took 37 buckets and pans to catch all the leaks. June and I covered our ears as she shouted, "Lucian Murphy, you have brought me to hell." This house happened to be on an east Texas oil lease.

But she never gave up on her decorating jobs. Someone lovingly remarked at her wake, "Thelma probably already has plans for redoing her own special cloud."

When she and Daddy finally bought a house for $60, Mama was as happy as if it were a mansion. It was her very OWN, her first one; and early spring found her redecorating another room. Her faith was firm, and I think having her own house helped to prove something to her.

Mama loved gardening and was proud of the fruits and vegetables she canned against the winter. Her specialty was "end-of-the-garden" soup. She would put the last of the vegetables—tomatoes, okra, beets, beans, carrots and onions-- into jars to make soup stock for cold winter nights.

The year Daddy bought a new-fangled gadget called a pressure cooker, he presented it to Mama with a big smile. This will make your job easier, Thelm', but don't try it till I get home from work. I'll need to help you till you get the hang of it." (That was like waving a red flag at a bull.)

Mama liked doing things herself. June and I helped with gathering and cleaning the vegetables; Mama put them in the jars and tightened down the lids. When she sent us outside, I reminded her, "Daddy said you shouldn't do this by yourself."

"Now ya'll go on out and play. There's nothing to this. I can handle it."

Later as I started into the kitchen, Mama began to yell, "Watch it! Don't come in! You'll cut your feet on the broken glass!" Tears glistened on her beet red cheeks.

Glass was everywhere and the ceiling was a veggie Picasso painting. "What happened, Mama? Are you OK?"

"Your daddy's gonna' kill me. That damn pressure cooker blew up! Get back outside and don't come back in."

Much later after Daddy came home from work, the kitchen had been cleaned. June and I stayed outside as Mama and Daddy "discussed" the vegetable explosion. Sometimes it got pretty loud. After it was over, Daddy left to get sandwiches for supper. Mama had nothing to say for the rest of the evening. In later years when we laughed about the soup explosion, Mama never joined in. She seemed to be needed elsewhere.

She did conquer that pressure cooker and, as years went by, canned many jars of vegetables. I'm not sure she ever put up soup again.

Later when the 'hot lunch' program came into the schools, Mama put her cooking skills to use again. The school needed cooks and Mama became known as the *pie lady*. She could whip out those pies in the wink of an eye and they were so-o-o good. And just think, the entire lunch was only ten cents. That included a big piece of Mrs. Murphy's pie.

Mama enjoyed sewing and could make Grandma's old treadle Singer really "sing." I'm not sure that June and I always appreciated her talent to be able to make a dress out of almost any piece of material including flour sacks.

One Monday morning, I gave her a real challenge when I announced at breakfast, "James and I are getting married next Sunday." (He was in the army, just another soldier on his way to Korea. He had two weeks leave so we decided the next Sunday would be a good time for a wedding.)

For once in his life, Daddy was speechless, but Mama swallowed hard, then said, "Well, it looks like I'm gonna' be pretty busy this week. Good thing you bought that moiré material here while back. It'll make a nice wedding dress."

I went on to my teacher's job; James went back to camp; Mama and Daddy went to work. Mama put the last covered button on my beautiful dress on Saturday night. Sunday afternoon friends from everywhere gathered at the church. My Uncle Bill brought Grandma down from Illinois. Brother John, James' dad, performed the ceremony, with the reception afterwards at a friend's house. I'll never know how they did it, but I heard later that everyone on the lease helped. Mama never quit smiling the whole time.

Later that same spring, like an unexpected tornado, a heart attack struck Daddy at work and took him from us. Mama was only 44 years old and for a while, it was as if she had left us too. Her eyes were filled with pain and she seemed like a lost child. She buried Daddy in the country cemetery in the little town in Illinois where they had grown up, then returned to the lease. She sold her $60 house for $600 and returned to Illinois to be near her family. Though neither June nor I agreed at the time, it later proved to be a good move.

Using Daddy's $5,000 insurance money, her four brothers and other relatives and friends built a brand new house for her in town. Truly, it was by far the nicest house she ever had. She started working in her brother's grocery store and, as she visited with all the customers and old friends, after a while, her grief softened. Through it all, Mama continued to live her life as she always had—with red dirt grit and determination.

One of the things special about Mama was that she always made herself available for others. She seemed to be able to step in and help them as needed.

In a few years. she found renewed happiness as a farmer's wife, till he, too, was gone. Once more a sadness settled over her spirit, but once more again she battled back and found a new direction for her life. At *only* 70 years of age, she began working at the local nursing home, and let us know she was "taking care of the old people."

Years later, dementia started playing tricks with her mind. One night during her last visit with me, I helped her get ready for bed. I started to leave the room as she crawled under the covers, and a little voice called out," Wait a minute."

I confess there was some frustration as I asked, "Yes. What do you want now, Mama?"

"Aren't you gonna' tuck me in?"

Properly chagrined, I turned, pulled the covers up and gave her a kiss. "Of course, Mama. Sleep tight, I love you."

For one of the very few times in my life, she whispered, "I love you, too." As I started down the hall, I heard her saying her prayers. "Please help me not to be 'mean' to other people."

By the time Mama reached 98 years, the dementia had almost won. Proving she was still in control, she told us that she was ready to go out to Clarksville to be with Daddy. Soon after, she went quietly to sleep.

The last time I saw her, the pain was smoothed away and a tiny smile played across her face. She had chosen the funeral herself, down to the last rose petal and a song that was perfect for Mama's life as she had lived it, "A Mansion Just Over The Hilltop."

"Oh, Mama, I needed just a little longer. In all our times together, there's something I always meant to tell you—how often I have looked to you for strength in living. As one of my friends said in loving memory, "You so truly were a Red Dirt Mama.""

An Ordinary Man

"**H**igher, Daddy! You gotta' push me higher! I wanna' touch those green leaves way up there."

"Stretch out your legs, Toots. You'll have to stretch out those legs if you <u>really</u> want to touch the highest leaves."

So I stretched--because this ordinary man told me to. He was stocky, swarthy and short. Every time the swing came down, he had to jump to catch the seat board for the forward push.

Just an ordinary oil-field worker having a great time at the annual Sinclair family picnic; certainly not a person to command a second glance--unless, by chance, the passerby happened to catch the intense fire in his eyes. There burned an eternal flame fueled by another question waiting for an answer, another puzzle waiting to be solved, another story waiting to be told.

This *ordinary* man was my daddy, and he taught me to live to the very edge of my being, to stretch for what waited out there.

People sometimes said, "You must be your Daddy's boy," because they knew my toys were a little different. Basketballs, footballs, roller skates, a BB gun, cowboy boots with a hat to wear--not exactly what a little girl of the early 40's might find under the Christmas tree.

Best of all, these presents carried a bonus. Because Daddy was a shiftworker at the gasoline plant, he was sometimes home during the day. He taught me the rules of the games: to put the ball through the hoop, catch the pass, get up after a fall, to shoot for the bull's eye; usually with a laugh and a word of encouragement, "Ok, let's give it another shot."

My favorite sport, girls' basketball, was very popular in Oklahoma schools. I really liked playing and because I attended a very small school, I did make the team, in spite of a couple of problems--I was only five feet tall and I really wasn't very good. Still, I did make a very good *bench-warmer*. "Stretch up," encouraged Daddy, "Play like you're tall." I practiced every day, learned to hang on to passes and tried to guard the forward's shots. Usually, when I got to play in the game, I was nervous but tried hard. It seemed to be almost enough. Of course, sometimes, I was really "ticked" because I didn't get to play more. "But you did your best, right?" You know where that was coming from. My answer was usually, "Yeah, I guess so."

One job was very special to me--side mechanic and tool handler, when Daddy worked on that old '37 Ford. Like a surgeon's assistant, I would pass the tools under the hood. "This needs a wrench." "How about a screwdriver?"

"We need to adjust this carburetor valve a little. We could use the gas mileage." He patiently explained the mysteries hidden there and I never had to pretend interest. I really did want to know; besides it was way, way better than dusting knick knacks or washing dishes.

With less than a high school education, Daddy's thirst for knowledge was never quite filled. He read anything available. When the fourth grade teacher thought reading aloud might help my reading skills, Daddy jumped at the chance to be the listener. I chose the book <u>Heidi</u> and read a chapter every day or so. Almost halfway through the book, I came home from school and there was Daddy, almost finished with the book.

"Daddy! What are you doing? I'm supposed to read to you."

"It's O.K. You know, Toots," laughed Daddy. "I couldn't wait to see what was going to happen to this little girl. Besides, the book is so good, I can hear it again." And he did.

Daddy was a spinner of yarns, and the tapestries he wove were filled with the colors of fun and excitement, and always people. His mother died at his birth, an aunt took him and loved him for six years, then Grandpa remarried an older woman hoping she would care for his three boys. Unfortunately, she never had a clue, but somehow they made it through.

The tales of growing up with aunts and uncles and cousins on the farms of central Illinois were always to be treasured. Later came the stories heard around the old coal stove in his father's country store. It was the gathering place on winter afternoons and as a boy, Daddy heard many stories that he retold later. A seed was planted in my heart. Perhaps, one day I could share stories that would cause people to laugh or cry, or see life in a *different* way.

The day he brought in a big package (surprises were great fun for him), I couldn't wait. "What in the world is this, Daddy?"

"Open it, you'll see."

I pulled off the brown paper, and there in a case was a guitar, actually taller than I--which, of course, wasn't really too tall. "What's this for?"

"Well, I thought you might like to learn to play it, so we can have a little music when we sing."

I think Daddy may have had thoughts of us becoming another *Carter Family* or maybe the *Stamps Quartet*. Of course, it never happened. I did learn to strum a few chords, and when the guy from the Oklahoma City radio station came to our little town looking for talent for a talent show, I asked Daddy if he thought my little sister and I might enter.

"Why not? You'll never know what you can do if you don't try."

We were accepted as contestants and June and I practiced for weeks. Our song was <u>Playmates, Come Out And Play With Me</u>. At four and eleven years old, we were pretty cute wearing our pinafores and new bonnets Mama had made for the contest. It would be the perfect ending if I could say, "We won first place," but we didn't. I think

even our second place win was because my sister's lisp captured the judges' hearts. She was quite the little flirt.

Later, I made a little confession to Daddy, "I know it's right that LaVerne won first place. Nobody plays the piano the way he does."

"You're right, Toots, but you know what I always say." "Yeah, Daddy, I know, and we did do our best, at least we tried."

"Then, never forget, that's what counts."

In the years I had him, Daddy taught me so many things about what counts--to be gentle with God's critters; to tend the flowers and vegetables; to respect all of God's creation; to run, but not forget to rest; to laugh, but cry when necessary and, above all, to remember the amazing love of Jesus.

He died at 46, and in the 23 years he was with me, I'm not sure he ever said the words, "I love you," but in every way, I never, ever doubted that he did. He truly cared about what I thought and what I did. He never talked 'to' me, he talked 'with' me; but even more, he listened, really listened, to what I thought about all kinds of things.

He helped me to see that beyond each star is another--a little higher, a little brighter and it CAN be reached. He gave me the courage to stretch upward with the confidence that it can be done.

A "small" ordinary man who gave me a giant gift for the ages--to live life to the very edge of my being. Thank you, Daddy, for pushing me higher.

Mommie, Please, A Penny For Peanuts?

If I hear a toddler ask this question, I want to say, "No, Mommie, you mustn't. Please, not now. Wait till that baby is older."

And why would I be so bold. Because my three-year-old asked me the same question with near tragic results. It remains as a painful memory even today

It started so innocently with a trip to Laundry Village. We'd been there longer than usual and after riding the pony, looking at the books, and taking a little nap, Donna was getting impatient. When she spotted the peanut machine, she asked the logical question.

With penny in hand, she went to "do it herself" and watched the peanuts fall down the chute. After popping them in her mouth, she ran back to me. On the way, she stumbled, choked a bit and gave a little cough. Before I could reach her, she seemed fine.

Later at home after her nap, I noticed she was wheezing a little. It had an asthmatic sound and that was strange because she'd never had asthma. For some reason I thought of the peanut. Feeling a little foolish, I called our family doctor to explain what had happened. "He asked a couple of questions. By now, it was late afternoon and he said, "Watch her, and we'll give her a little time. If she's still wheezing in the morning, bring her in."

By morning, the wheezing had increased until I could hear her from one room to the other. She was running a low-grade fever and I had waited long enough. We were on our way to the doctor's office.

Although the X-ray revealed very little (keep in mind this happened many years ago), our doctor made arrangements for her to be admitted to the pediatric wing at the hospital (about 40 miles away) under a specialist's care. I tried to convince my bouncy toddler that even though she'd had one nap, she needed to hop into bed again. Even with all the wheezing she remained very active.

As I listened to the explanations, the peanut became the enemy. The specialist explained the danger of peanuts for any child under the age of four. (At that time, peanuts led all other foods and objects to be aspirated throughout the world. Not only did the danger come from the peanut, but the oil was especially noxious to the lung with pneumonia as a secondary threat.)

The weapons to be used against this "enemy" were to perform a bronchoscopy procedure to fish the peanut our of the bronchi and to start antibiotics to fight the pneumonia, should it develop. The doctor commended us that we had not stuck a finger in Donna's throat when she choked, due to the danger of impacting the peanut into the larynx.

It was decided to perform the bronchoscopy early the next morning. James was working the midnight shift; he left to make arrangements for our sons (ages 5 and 7), get some sleep, and return to the hospital the next morning.

After Donna ate some supper, she went to sleep and I sat in the white rocker by her bed, listening to every breath she took--in and out, pause, in and out. Finally I left to go to my sister's nearby apartment to get some rest myself.

Early the next morning I returned to the hospital to find that Donna was beginning to show some fear. The little boy in the bed next to hers was eating breakfast. She had none and she wasn't too happy about that.

When they came for her to go to surgery, she wouldn't get on the cart, so I carried her, down the hall, into the elevator and down another hall. Little girls can be very strong at times! I had to force her arms from around my neck, and with help laid her on the cart. I put her ragged old blanket on top of her, and tried to shut out her cries as I watched the doors to surgery swing shut behind her.

I went to the little waiting room to sit and wait and pray. I thought of so many things: memories of Donna's first three years. James came sooner than I expected and it was a little easier as we continued our wait together.

Several cups of coffee later, the doors finally opened and a smiling doctor came out. He showed us the peanut. now crushed into pieces in a pan of water. It had been caught halfway down in the right lung, and had to be fragmented to be removed.

I gave him a hug, and said, "Now it's over."

"Not quite. Now we wait."

There would be swelling from the bronchoscope rubbing on her tiny throat. The next five hours would be critical. A tracheotomy could become necessary.

When we reached her room, Donna was placed in a croupette where a mixture of oxygen and mist was forced through crushed ice into a plastic tent. This helped ease her breathing.

She seemed so tiny and lay so still. I kept thinking, "If she would only move a little." I knew she was receiving the best possible care, as the three doctors kept coming in checking her. The clock ticked on and we waited.

At last she stirred a little, then opened her brown eyes. Her thin whisper came like music as she croaked, "Water, Mommie."

Children can adjust so quickly. With only a little fussing, she accepted her cold, damp tent for the next 24 hours.

The next day the secondary "enemy forces" appeared and I *saw* pneumonia. The pediatrician pointed out on the X-ray the gray circles running along the inside of the right lung. One plus--the peanut had apparently been stale and had lost some of its oil because the inflammation was only partial. I felt very grateful that the vending company had not changed its peanuts too often.

Soon there was definite improvement; Donna began to beg to go home. She even mentioned missing her brothers. After five days, the doctors agreed she would be happier at home and she was released. She returned to the hospital each week for five weeks to be checked.

As the doctor filled out her final dismissal papers he said, "No more peanuts for this little lady for quite awhile."

"Hm--more like never," I thought.

Who would have thought that an innocent little peanut could have caused so much dangerous havoc. Mommies, do be careful of your toddlers at the peanut machine! Please!!

Less Than An Eagle —
More Than A Duck

Quiet darkness sent the first clue. No light in the hall. No TV cowboys riding in the distance. No pungent smell of morning coffee luring me out of bed. Just silence! "Something is wrong--very, very wrong!"

Throwing back the covers, I called, "James, where are you?"

"I need you." The slurred words sounded a second clue.

I stumbled over my husband lying on the living room floor, the third clue.

"Can this be a stroke?" The whispered prayer came without thinking, "Lord, please help me to think."

James mumbled, "Get me up, just get me up." I tried, but his whole left side had turned to stone--nothing moved. "Just get me to a chair," he pleaded. "I'll rest a minute before I go to work."

I had no choice. Leaving him on the floor, I ran to dial the magic numbers--911. Almost before I could pull on my clothes, our small-town rescue squad was coming through the door. These self-assured young men went right to work and were soon ready to leave for the hospital.

"Follow us!" As they lifted him into the rescue vehicle, James urged me, "Bring my truck. I'll go to work from the hospital."

"Not today," I thought. Little did I know how many months would pass before he would 'go to work'.

The first day blurred into a hodgepodge of tests and phone calls. Nurses shuttled in and out. I watched for some kind of movement on

James' left side, "Please, God, just any sign that the stone is crumbling." Only a rigid stillness hid under the cover.

The confusion in James' eyes increased as he struggled to understand. December, 1987. Throughout the day I watched the snow swirling by the window. "Dear Lord," I begged, "what *is* happening to us?"

As time dragged on, I sat by the bed, clinging to that rigid hand. Donna, our daughter, arrived, fearful, but comforting. Pastor Bill came and prayed with us. About nine o'clock that night, a doctor (the first one) finally appeared.

He confirmed my predawn fear--a massive stroke **had** occurred. After a little talk, the doctor urged me to go home and get some rest.

"Go home? What do you mean 'go home?' No way!" James was so restless. Surely there's something I can do. The doctor assured me the best way I could help was to prepare for tomorrow. There would be no more treatments tonight. (This was in the pre clot-buster days and even if it had been available, we were already past those critical early-hours for that treatment.) With one final kiss, I left.

Only our great, white sled dogs were waiting for me when I entered the cold, empty house. As I sank to the floor and buried my face in their soft fur, I remembered my unread morning devotional. I turned the pages and the Psalmist's words raced round and round in my head. "Give me strength; I am completely exhausted and my whole being is deeply troubled." Surely these words were for me, "Give me strength, give me strength." Misti and Tasha licked the first tears of the day that were streaming down my face.

Another dawn, and I followed another ambulance moving James to the neurological intensive care unit of another hospital. His room was a scene from some TV medical drama with machines beeping and drip tubes puncturing his veins. Still no answers for James' bewildered questioning look. I was still waiting for answers myself. Where was the neurologist?

So many decisions waiting. Both our sons were working offshore--Rick on an aircraft carrier in the Atlantic and John on a diving barge in the Gulf of Mexico. Donna and I were torn with the question. "Do we cut through the red tape immediately to get in touch with them? Or do we wait, especially since we had so few answers." After calling their wives, we chose to follow their thinking and wait a few days.

Finally, on Saturday night I connected with James' neurologist and I felt my first glimmer of hope. Things were *very* serious, but the doctor reassured me, "James has had his stroke; we've passed the life-threatening point. We're at the bottom of the mountain--now we can start climbing."

Sunday morning. Was it really only four days since that shattering morning? With some reluctance, I entered my home church braced for more questions and I prepared to gulp down tears. But during the service, I felt a bold reassurance that James and I COULD begin the journey before us. I knew the Lord was with us, because I felt our church family surrounding us with their loving concern and prayers. As time passed, these loving people became an integral part of our recovery.

I John 3:18 became my touchstone, "My children, our love should not be just words and talk; it must be true love, which shows itself in action."

During those 14 days in NICU and 61 days when James worked so hard in his twice-a-day therapy sessions at the Rehab Hospital, we were continually uplifted by God's love through his wonderful 'children of action'.

The first card we received was from one who wrote, "I said a prayer for you today and here is what I had to say, 'Dear Lord, please make Mr. Jim better; make him whole in every way. I know that he's a worker, Lord, and he won't complain one word, but he surely can use your help, the strong, unending help that only You afford. Help my friend follow to the letter each and every nudge You offer. He will respond, he's no quitter. Thank you dear Lord, for listening.'"

There were so many others. . .

. . . The nurse who helped James with his transfer to Rehab that snowy day, who gave him a hug and smiled through her tears, "I just love you, Mr. Dennis. You're going to make it and I'll pray for you every day."

. . . Friends who made it possible for James to come home for visits before he could even stand. They helped with the transfers from car to house to car and in other ways.

. . . The Sunday School class whose birthday balloons set an all-time record for cheerfulness--55 days in the hospital and 60 more days at home before they even started to droop. One of them had a smiley face and James assured me that someone on the hospital ceiling was smiling at him each night while I was gone.

. . . The Rehab staff who arranged our surprise anniversary cake.

. . . The diamond-in-the-rough kind of guy who turned as he left one night to smile, "Keep on prayin', Mrs. D. My grandma says it works, and I know it does."

. . . A very special love-in-action person like Wendy, who had dinner waiting for me night after night, no matter how late I came home from the hospital. Who later provided therapy taxi service week after week, so that I might continue my teaching obligations.

. . . Friends from all over the country who phoned, sent cards and bookmarks, wrote touching, encouraging, loving letters and said in every possible way, "Hang in there, you guys are tough. We're praying for you." And they were. Sometimes, before I would go to sleep, I would feel myself wrapped in a blanket of their love.

. . . Later, the amazing strangers who came up to us in grocery stores, at the pool, the mall, in restaurants, in all kinds of places and shared, "You've had a stroke, haven't you? So did my mother, my father, my wife, my uncle, etc. You're doing so *good*. Just keep on trying. That's the secret." A bond of strength seems to connect all stroke patients and their families no matter who they are or where they are.

Every whispered prayer of individuals and prayer chains scattered across a dozen states sustained and strengthened us. We celebrated an answer to these prayers when James' big toe **finally** moved back and forth on command--a tiny crack in that stone-hard left side.

We celebrated James' sixtieth birthday on December 23 at the Rehab Center with our kids. Christmas was another story. Because our children were scattered, we'd planned for over a year to have a family Christmas together for the first time in eight years.

Friends said, "What a shame that James can't come home for Christmas." I knew better. I put it into God's hands, then helped all I could by begging the doctors. "Please, you have to make it possible for him to be home with us, if only for a little while."

Rick and John, our sons, spent a day in physical therapy learning how to make this happen. God answered our prayers Christmas morning as the boys wheeled their dad through the front door. As we celebrated the birth of the baby Jesus, we celebrated James' homecoming. Only a few hours, but he was home and it was a day of joy and giving thanks. As I looked around at my children and grandchildren, at my mother and my dear husband, it was the very best Christmas of my life.

Several days later, the first 'day pass' made me very nervous. Christmas was over, the family was gone; I was on my own. The physical therapist had taught me a lot, especially transferring to and from the wheelchair, a big deal for stroke patients. Still, on the way home, I informed James that we would NOT try the bathroom transfer; so if the need came up, he would have to wait till we returned to the hospital which was about an hour from us.

We settled in for our few hours together. It was New Year's Day, we had lunch and watched ballgames. So far so good. Then, of course, you know what happened. James said he <u>couldn't</u> wait. He had to go to the bathroom NOW! There was no way I could dissuade him, so we transferred to the wheelchair, wheeled down the hall--got up, pulled, steadied, pivoted, swayed, almost fell, recovered and at last, he was in place with no disastrous happenings.

I danced around shouting, "Yea, we made it, we made it, we can do it! Hooray!" Then I realized James was very quiet. "What? We made it!"

He looked up at me and sighed, "But, honey, you forgot to pull my pants down." Properly humbled, we started over.

The snows of winter dragged on. I went to school, to the hospital, came home, fed the dogs, checked the mail and each morning everything started over. As time passed, James' foot and leg slowly began to respond to the therapy. While Michelle (his astonishing physical therapist) steadied him with the safety belt, he walked a few steps. Little by little his confidence grew, and a cane was added. It did <u>not</u> replace the wheelchair yet, but it gave us hope when it could be used for a few steps.

Hitting his mouth with a spoonful of food was another goal he worked on. But when it came to food, James was pretty handy. And except for soup, he managed most things pretty well.

One frustrating fact remained--no matter how hard everyone tried, the left arm was still a stone, moving only with spasmodic jerks. (No matter how many times I lift it during our therapy time, it remains the same, even to this very day.)

On February 16, the doctor had a different greeting for me. "Mrs. Dennis, I think tomorrow you can take James home. He will continue outpatient therapy three times a week." (Could this be really true?) We went over endless details, and the next afternoon, we said a final goodbye to the nurses.

. . . and our new life began!

Always the agonizing question remains. "Why? Why did this happen to *us?*" All my thinking is wrapped around us. Stroke is a family affair and touches the whole family. Accepting this concept is the beginning of understanding. Truthfully, I don't know why this happened to us, but this I do know. Over the 25 years since James managed to get through the door that meant home, we've discovered many things. (The doctor tried to prepare me in several ways, but I found I could only live it.) Frustration, a lot of anger and misunderstanding became a part of learning to live together in a new way.

Those first months we were learning and growing and shouting more at each other than in all of our first 37 years together. James' trust had been shattered. It wasn't easy for me to be patient with his need to control his own life. As a natural-born caregiver, I was overprotective and over-afraid. I knew I was wrong, I couldn't seem to help myself. James knew he was wrong to say hurtful words and not to trust me, but he couldn't seem to help himself.

When our feelings have been damaged again and again, we've had to back away and give it to the Lord--again. He's never turned us down.

The good times far outweigh the bad. One encouraging part is that even though some people say, "After six months, the improvement stops," that's just not true. Don't ever, ever give up and resign yourself that a stroke patient doesn't keep moving ahead. It may be in 'baby steps' but for us, it hasn't stopped.

After that first toe wiggle, foot and leg movement slowly continued. One day, many months later, I found James standing by the kitchen door, his cane pushed against the cabinet. I started toward him, but he said, "Wait." Step by step he walked toward me. Using all my willpower, I managed to wait. When he reached me, we grabbed each other and held on, laughing and crying. It's only by God's grace that we didn't both fall in the floor.

We do so take life for granted. That first morning I wakened to the smell of fresh coffee was a milestone I'll always remember. James had always been the coffee maker. We forget what happiness a simple joy can be. Try to imagine what it meant to James when, after years of trying, he discovered he could "spit and whistle" again.

Because stroke is a leading cause of serious long-term disability, falls are a constant threat and the risk increases as one ages. This is even more true for an adventurer like James. We've traveled extensively and it would seem we've probably recorded a fall in every state, except Alaska (maybe because we haven't been there yet). Because of overworked guardian angels, we have escaped a serious injury.

Emotions can jump off track at a moment's notice and leave James trembling in tears. Anger can be triggered like an erupting volcano, causing embarrassment and regret. We deal with these emotions as best we can. I am grateful that most people seem to understand. Recently we finally talked with the doctor about these problems and made an amazing discovery. There is help for this chemical imbalance and after trying the medication, it's as if I have my "real" husband back. A side benefit is that this makes me much easier to live with.

Perhaps this has been the greatest insight for me in this ongoing saga of life. Finally, I'm beginning to get a glimmer of the way God uses each of us to help others. Sometimes, in the midst of pain and confusion and even new health issues, receiving or giving that help may be very difficult, but the Lord cares for us in ways far beyond our meager understanding.

As our fiftieth wedding anniversary approached, I wanted to do something to let all the people who had been with us on our journey know what they had meant to us. We gave a party. What a party! We used Lee Ann Womack's song I Hope You Dance as our theme.

James had never, ever danced in his life, but before our friend sang that special song, she urged, "You MUST dance!" We did! James put his cane aside, and with his arms around me, we began to sway along.

As he held me, I thought, "So many said he would never walk again. Well, just take a look; we may not be soaring like eagles, but we're surely flying higher than ducks!"

Epilogue

In the ten years since that party, we have continued to live our life at the highest level possible. Still a little higher than the ducks, but a little slower. One of the best parts is that we still are able to travel this beautiful country, visit our relatives and friends, and we haven't missed a HIGH SCHOOL reunion in years. Last spring we celebrated my 65th year of graduation. That's another joy for which we thank God.

The Seasons of Love

In the seasons of living, James and I began our journey in the spring of our love--and we thought we had forever. It was new and exciting, and though sudden storms swept across our horizons, and though we were an ocean apart; we were together in our faith for the future.

In the summer of our love, with our three precious gifts to care for, no day seemed ever quite long enough, no task seemed ever quite completed. So much teaching, so much learning, so much living. It was still new, even more exciting; and we were still together in our hope for the future. We had a faith to fuel that hope.

Then one day, sooner than we could possibly imagine, a hint of gold has touched the leaves and we have now entered the autumn of our love. Our family continues to grow and we have discovered a wonderful truth--the well of love is fed by a stream that never runs dry. Yet, in this time of living we have found that storms still build in the west. As they come, they can be fierce and they can leave great devastation behind; but we have also found that with faith and hope and the love of God, our love for each other continues to be new and exciting and forever is still out there.

The Master Teacher says "For everything there is a season," and so we know that one day the lush colors of autumn will begin to fade. One by one, the leaves will float to the ground. But in God's plan for living, there is still a certain beauty to be found in the winter of our love.

During our wedding ceremony fifty years ago, Dad said to us, "Remember, two shall become as one; the family that prays together stays together." So surrounded by friends and family, today we joyously reaffirm those vows, knowing that our marriage has been grounded in a certain, sure knowledge--there abides faith, hope and love--and the greatest of these is love. Love of friends, love of family and love of God.

Well, Papaw, through the years we have tried to follow your advice the best that we can. The two of us are still becoming as one, and now we know this is more than forever; this is **eternal**!

—Written and read by Millie during the Vows Renewal ceremony 02/02/02

For Emmett
(A Red-dirt Lease Kid)

My path and Emmett's kind of crisscrossed throughout our whole lives. We lived within two or three miles of each other on the Seminole, OK oil leases, but never knew each other. Of course, that was in the late 1930's, and we were just little kids getting our lives started.

Later Emmett's dad opened a grocery store in Cherry Hill (about 20 miles away) and my family moved to Cherry Hill just about "spittin' distance" from the store. The problem was that Emmett's family had moved the summer before.

Emmett graduated from Bowlegs, OK and I graduated from Saint Louis, OK. The schools were about 25 miles apart and they played football against each other. Emmett says he remembers playing in Saint Louis at least once. But again there was no contact.

After graduation, Emmett married, had children and lived an exciting life all over the world as an FBI agent and a Diplomatic Security Agent in the Foreign Service, U.S. Department of State. I married, had children and lived an *exciting* life as a wife, mother and teacher all over central USA. Again our paths never crossed. . .

UNTIL . . . I wrote a book, <u>It's Gonna Be OK</u> and had a book signing in Seminole. The book was about growing up on the oil leases, and Emmett was curious, so he came and it happened--we finally met. Since then, we've had great times remembering the *olden days*, comparing thoughts on the current days; and generally, building our friendship with very occasional visits and frequent Emails. Emmett still calls Oklahoma home and I live in Ohio.

Emmett has been so encouraging since the day we met, and when I told him I was writing a new book, he Emailed, "Go for it." And so I am.

"Emmett, I am so thankful for our friendship, and want you to be a part of *this* undertaking. Thank you. Millie (another red-dirt lease kid)

About the Author

For over sixty years, MIldred Dennis has been answering the urge to write. Using an award winning newspaper column in Illinois and Ohio, three published inspirational books and numerous magazine articles as her outlets, she covered topics from the ups and downs of family living, to the rewards and problems of teaching, to a continuing love affair with all of nature and a sustaining faith in Jesus Christ.

As a Methodist layspeaker and a leader of seminars focusing on Christian beliefs and building self-image, Mrs. Dennis has had the opportunity to interact with hundreds of people. She taught 35 years in Oklahoma, Illinois and Ohio high school classrooms, winning awards as an outstanding teacher in the the English Arts and secretarial field.

She and James, husband of 61 years, grew up in in Oklahoma and now live in NE Ohio. Three adult children live in Alabama, Arizona and Ohio.

Her most recent book, "It's Gonna Be OK", tells of living on the Oklahoma and Texas oil leases during the 30s and 40s from childhood through young adulthood. This 'red-dirt' experience has had a lasting influence in her life and helped to form her personal values and enduring faith in God.

The book is a collection of ideas, columns and talks taken from the author's wealth of experiences through years of living. From "A Winter's Crystal Morning" through "Less Than An Eagle, More Than A Duck" the reader can spend a few minutes or a few hours sharing the joys and sad times of an everyday life blessed by Jesus Christ.